ABOMINATION  OF DESOLATION

THE APOSTATE CHURCH

Is Christianity based on devotion to Christ or a denomination?

MONICA BENNETT-RYAN

IN HIS NAME
PUBLISHING

PUBLISHED IN AUSTRALIA

THE APOSTATE CHURCH

ISBN: 978-0-6457906-6-5

IN HIS NAME
PUBLISHING
www.inhisname.com.au

Cover Design & Graphic Art

MONICA BENNETT-RYAN
© 2025 Monica Bennett-Ryan

Photography

BRONWEN RUSSELL
www.bronsdesign.com.au

All rights reserved solely by the author. No part of this book may be reproduced under any other name or for any purpose other than originally intended by the author without permission in writing from the publisher.

Scripture references are checked for accuracy through The Bible Hub. Historical observations derive from widely published historical facts.

Free for download through Kindle Unlimited. Also available in Ebook, Paperback and Hardcover. Direct any enquiries to: editor@inhisname.com.au

If anyone wants
to serve me,
he must follow me.

- John 2:26 -

CONTENTS

INTRODUCTION   7
It's your call!

CHAPTER 1   17
The First Christians

CHAPTER 2   29
A Political Solution

CHAPTER 3   45
Living Sacrifices

CHAPTER 4   69
A New Clergy Class

CHAPTER 5   81
Legacy Of Lies

CHAPTER 6   95
The Lord's Table

CHAPTER 7   107
The Anathema

CHAPTER 8   125
Standing For God

CHAPTER 9   149
Cancerous Apostasy

CHAPTER 10   163
Deceptive Tribunes

CHAPTER 11   173
A Spiritual Cure

CHAPTER 12   193
The Reputation Trap

CHAPTER 13   207
Christ's Way

CHAPTER 14   219
Sending Women

CHAPTER 15   233
Testing The Spirits

CHAPTER 16   245
Life Without Pulpits

THE AUTHOR   255
Why I wrote this book...

Christ or Religion?

INTRODUCTION

Two roads,
one important
choice!

IT'S YOUR CALL

This book will inspire everyone. Some will be so moved that they will want to throw the book into the fire and gather their pitchforks. Others will receive the message like a cool drink of water in the desert and praise God for the water. Either way, this book will make every reader think about one thing.

Am I a follower of Christ?

Most people who believe themselves to be Christian have been taught from pulpit after pulpit that being part of a denomination makes them a Christian, yet that's only true if Christianity is seen as a mere club that anyone can join. So, does being a member of one of the hundreds of Christian clubs automatically make the club members followers of Christ or merely part of the apostate church system? That's the question, isn't it?

The official definition of apostate is *one who renounces a religious belief or principle*, and this book explains why that definition is relevant to the religion that has come to be known as Christiantiy.

This book will challenge the presumption that belonging to a Christian denomination with its endless schedules of religious activities makes its members followers of Christ. It will encourage everyone to question whether their personal idea of Christianity is based on devotion to Christ or to their denomination—two very different things.

THE OLD WORLD ORDER   THE NEW WORLD ORDER

On the front cover is the emblem of the Roman Empire, whose driving force was world domination. The biggest thorn in the side of their quest for world domination was what they termed 'the problem of religion', particularly the indomitable new sect known as 'followers of The Way'. For centuries, they tried every cruel and sadistic means of dissuading this sect, but nothing worked until one Emperor, Constantine, formulated a brilliant idea.

He would use this group to his own advantage and the advantage of the Roman Empire. It would become the basis of his new State-run religion, inclusive of all religions, but with its leadership firmly under his control. The core of that control would become known as the pulpit.

It's no accident that the emblem of the New World Order, currently trying to bring the various religions of the world under their rigid control, resembles the emblem of the Roman Empire. It's basically the same organisation repackaged, and their goal is still world domination.

Will they also use the pulpit?

Despite what people have been led to believe about pulpits, they were set up as the central control system of a new pseudo-religion to keep all religious adherents submissive to the State. They were the basis of Constantine's new Roman Universal Church, the only recognised religion of the Roman Empire and all its conquered lands.

It didn't matter to Constantine that he was setting up a fake religion that could only promote pretence and hypocrisy. His motive for forming this pseudo-religion was political. He wanted to bring religion, with all its rivalry and sacrificial blood-letting, under government control. There was no faith involved.

Piety or pretence?

There have always been pretenders in churches. Wolves in sheep's clothing, false prophets and manipulated doctrines have always been around. Christ warned us about wolves, false prophets and the 'leaven' (false doctrine) of the Pharisees, and Paul warned us about pretenders in the churches. But Constantine made false doctrine and pretenders in pulpits the basis of his new religion.

Jesus told them. "Beware of the leaven of the Pharisees and Sadducees". Matthew 16:6

My life has been in danger in cities, in deserts, at sea, and with people who only pretended to be the Lord's followers. 2 Corinthians 11:26

God allows the deception!

This book will unfold the battle that Constantinian religion has been waging against the genuine Way of Christ for centuries, and how God Himself has ultimately set them up for failure. Pretenders in pulpits typically know they are there to 'lord' it over God's people, oppose Christ's stated will, stand between people and God, encourage disobedience and become rich at the expense of God's poor. However, the wickedness they promote is limited by God's decree. The planned obstacles, controls and cunning manipulations they unleash can never affect the genuine followers of Christ, for God only allows those dark forces to work on people who do not love His Son with their whole hearts.

> *The coming lawlessness will be accompanied by the activity of Satan and directed against those who are perishing, because they refused to love the truth that would have saved them.*
>
> *For this reason God will send them a powerful delusion so that they believe the lie, in order that judgment may come upon all who have disbelieved the truth and delighted in wickedness. 2 Thessalonians 2:9-12*

God has allowed a certain amount of wicked deception to be taught to those who are already perishing, that is, non-believers, religious 'club' Christians and outright pretenders. But the lies of 'lords' in pulpits will not fool those who love Christ and are prepared to follow him, even to death. They are the genuine believers, who walk the narrow way.

Small is the gate
and narrow is
the way
that leads to life,
and only a few find it.

- Matthew 7:13-14 -

The Way of Christ!

CHAPTER 1

Separating
the real
followers of Christ
from the fakes
and the pretenders!

THE FIRST CHRISTIANS

Paul's words about the coming of lawlessness were written well before the full effect of the lawlessness he described could be seen, but because of his warning, it was easily recognisable when it came.

And it was bad!

The first evidence of its coming was widespread martyrdom and persecution. So we see that for 275 years after Christ's death, followers of The Way were viciously tortured, persecuted and treated as threats to society. They were boiled in oil, thrown to lions, crucified, sawn in two, covered in pitch and lit as torches, wrapped in animal skins and thrown to dogs, torn apart by horses, beaten to death, beheaded, mutilated and killed in gladiator games.

Peter and Paul died in this purge!

Not every believer was martyred during this prolonged oppression. Some were imprisoned, exiled, had their homes, property and possessions confiscated, were refused work, deprived of public office and civil rights, or seduced with bribes. Most of the killings and persecutions were done because the followers of Christ refused to worship the various Emperors of Rome or acknowledge their deity by calling them 'lord'. Such refusal was seen as the cause of all natural disasters, like floods, famines, plagues, fires, droughts, and even social unrest.

Followers of The Way of Christ also refused to tolerate widely accepted pagan practices and so were seen as a threat to society. In response, they were forbidden on pain of death to encourage anyone to follow Christ. Yet, despite this great bloodbath of hate, constant persecutions, and severe limitations, the followers of Christ grew in faith and number.

Why was that?

The secret to their success was Christ's Great Commission. His followers took him at his word, accepted his command, and obeyed him. They knew they had his authority to preach the Gospel, baptise, heal the sick, and cast out demons. They knew they didn't need any human permission to obey Christ. Their simple obedience was accompanied by the miraculous in ways that even Romans couldn't deny.

> *They went out and preached everywhere, and the Lord worked through them, confirming His word by signs that accompanied it. Mark 16:20*
>
> *God did extraordinary miracles through the hands of Paul, so that even handkerchiefs and aprons that had touched him were taken to the sick, and the diseases and evil spirits left them. Acts 19:11-12*
>
> *A sense of awe came over everyone, and the apostles performed many wonders and signs. Acts 2:43*
>
> *My message and my preaching were not with persuasive words of wisdom, but with a demonstration of the Spirit's power, so that your faith would not rest on men's wisdom, but on God's power. 1Corinthians 2:4-5*

His Commission is his Way!

The Gospel, accompanied by signs and wonders, was Christ's Way, and now it is our Way. His Great Commission is his command to us and, therefore, is not negotiable! This is how all followers of Christ must follow him. This is the Way! There is no other!

Time hasn't changed this command. Despite being relegated by pretenders to *'The Age Of The Apostles'* (as if there were such a thing), there is no evidence anywhere in Scripture that this command was ever revoked or will be revoked. If it hasn't been revoked, it is still in effect and every person who claims that Christ is Lord is expected to obey this command and fulfil his Great Commission.

> *Why do you call me 'Lord, Lord,' but do not do what I say? Luke 6:46*

Empowered by God's Spirit!

Christ's chosen way of spreading his Gospel can't be done by human power alone. All the works he has commissioned us to do must be done by God's own Spirit. If they are not done by the power of God's Holy Spirit, they won't be effective.

This is why the first disciples, their disciples, and centuries of all of their following disciples were so effective. For hundreds of years, The Way of Christ continued to rapidly grow in number despite constant threats of horrific persecution and death.

God's Spirit is key!

The first disciples went out into the world and preached the Gospel of Salvation to all who would listen. Men, women and children made disciples wherever they went. By the power of the Spirit of God, they baptised them, healed those who were sick, cast out any demons, raised the dead, laid hands on all of them for the infilling of the Spirit and then commissioned them to go out into the world and give as they had received. They taught everyone to go and make disciples in obedience to the Great Commission of Christ.

This was the recognised work of the Holy Spirit through every disciple, every believer, and every follower of Christ, whether young or old, rich or poor, male or female, and it was deliberately unstructured. Instead, it was based on prayer and fasting, and all the 'going' was led by the Spirit.

They partnered with God!

For hundreds of years, the followers of Christ worked with the Spirit of God as Christ had demonstrated. They watched for God to begin the work and then worked with him to complete it. They were flexible and not bound to one place, but could go where the Spirit led them at any time. They did not try to control God; they allowed God to control them. They understood that this was God's work, not theirs and all praise for everything achieved would go to Him, not them.

They shared testimony!

When they gathered together, it was not in specially built churches, but in homes or public spaces, like a town square or a covered outdoor area, and their meetings were unstructured. The main purpose of coming together was to hear testimony and encourage further ministry. Filled with joy, new followers needed to share the miraculous things they'd seen God do, how He'd filled their minds with understanding or proven His word through miracles or answered their prayers or met their spiritual or practical needs. And everyone had a chance to share their wonderful testimonies to God's glory!

That was fellowship!

The place didn't matter; it was the opportunity to share what God had done that mattered. What they had seen God do in them and through them filled them with rejoicing. When others testified, their joy erupted into praise. But knowing they could be partners with God as He did his work on earth filled them with awe. This awe-filled joy was something they could not explain; it had to be experienced, and it fueled their desire to share this astoundingly profound good news with as many as possible.

And the Gospel spread!

The entire New Testament is filled to the brim with testimony after testimony to the glorious work of the Spirit through Christ and those who followed His Way.

They grew in number!

As the early disciples grew in number, it became apparent that something needed to be organised for the thousands of joyous new believers who had begun regularly gathering together in various places. They wanted somewhere to bring their gifts and share fellowship around a common meal. So the disciples prayed and came up with a solution.

When you come together, each of you has a hymn, or a word of instruction, a revelation, a tongue or an interpretation. Everything must be done so that the church may be built up. 1 Corinthians 4:26

The early church was given a recipe for spiritual nurture and growth. It allowed all followers, men, women, and children, to share testimonies, bring a spiritual message, sing whatever song was on their heart, share a recent revelation of truth, or proclaim a prophetic word. These gatherings, which included eating a meal, took hours.

Whether these gatherings were in homes or larger public spaces, it became clear that some people should be set aside to 'wait on tables' and ensure everyone had what they needed, like food and drinks, while everyone else took the time to testify or share how God was leading them.

Christ showed his disciples how to conduct their gatherings so that God's Spirit could move freely among His people.

The leaders were servants!

The first seven people chosen for leadership roles in the gatherings of believers were men of the day who were 'filled with the Spirit' and had proven they could follow the Spirit's leading.

> The twelve disciples gathered all the other disciples and said, "It would not be right for us to neglect the ministry of the word of God in order to wait on tables...choose seven men from among you...and we will turn this responsibility over to them". Acts 6:2-4

The Apostles sat at the tables with all the other disciples and supervised as everyone learned how to share their testimonies and revelations and submit to the leading of the Spirit. They didn't act as overlords but as equals in the work of the ministry of the Gospel.

They didn't get paid!

All the offerings, including food, drink, clothing, precious oils, houses, furniture, parcels of land and money, were brought to the disciples, who did not keep what was offered or even take a wage. Instead, the offerings received were immediately distributed among those in their gatherings who had need, and no one went without. These offerings were given to God, and the disciples rightly treated them as holy.

We see the holy attitude the disciples had toward donated offerings in the story of the healing of the man begging in front of the temple.

Peter and John spoke the truth when they told this lame man they had no money, but what they had to offer him was far better than money could buy.

> *Peter said, "Silver or gold I do not have, but what I have I give you: In the name of Jesus Christ of Nazareth, get up and walk!" Acts 3:6*

How far we have fallen!

The expectations of Christians today have fallen so far below that understanding of the power of the Spirit of God at work in us that most of us can't imagine seeing this kind of healing in our own lifetime. And yet, the Gospel hasn't changed, the Great Commission hasn't changed, and the ability of God's Spirit to work through us hasn't changed.

So, what has changed?

> *They triumphed over him (Satan) by the blood of the Lamb and by the word of their testimony. And did not love their lives so much as to shrink from death. Revelation 12:11*

For hundreds of years, the followers of The Way of Christ triumphed so effectively over the brutal treatment they received on the orders of various Roman Emperors that, in the end, Rome finally conceded that persecution was not going to stop the spread of the Gospel. They concluded that they would, therefore, need to find another means of control.

And they did!

All authority in
heaven and earth
has been given
to me,
therefore go
and make disciples.

- Matthew 28:18-19 -

State Intervention!

CHAPTER 2

Pulpits were
erected
to restrict the
Great Commission!

A POLITICAL SOLUTION

It was obvious that the Great Commission had to be contained, and what better way to contain it than to take Christ's Commission out of the people's hands and place it into the hands of the Emperor? After all, the singular purpose of the Roman Empire was world domination, and this religious 'commission' could become very useful if handled correctly.

But what could be done?

These followers of Christ had no particular religious structure. Unlike all the other existing religions, they did not meet to offer sacrifices. They were known to talk about their God wherever they were: at home, in the marketplace, even in the Colosseum. It seemed that the whole world was their temple, with every day dedicated to serving their God. Moreover, they refused to acknowledge the Emperor as god. That had to change! And so a method of restricting these wayward Christ lovers and forcing them to use their religious zeal in the service of the Emperor began to take shape.

State-controlled religion!

Constantine, the 55th Emperor of Rome, was determined to make a name for himself. He now saw that solving the massive problem of religion and its factional tensions would be his ticket to fame and immortality. And he had a plan!

> He would not just control one religion, he would control all of them!

He envisioned a unified, one-world religion. A religion without the blood-letting of animals. A religion that would include elements of all the other religions. A religion that he could control and use in the conquering of nations. But best of all, a religion that would bow to him and give him the homage every Emperor/Caesar/Pontiff of Rome deserved.

And so it began!

Rome's Soldiers: For centuries, Rome's soldiers had been kept busy policing the volatile differences between religions in the various nations they had conquered. It was one thing to go into battle to conquer, but the spoils of war did not come with policing. The constant executions and brutal punishments they were forced to inflict on the enemies of the State were hugely demoralising.

> With this solution, Rome's soldiers could be a conquering army again.

The Streets: The sickening stench of rotten blood from the ritualistic killing of sacrificial animals filled the air. There was always some animal being sacrificed to some god somewhere. The foul-smelling aroma was a constant source of annoyance to Constantine, and this was his chance to eliminate the problem.

> With this solution, the streets could be made beautiful and enjoyable.

The Altars: As their last act of religious policing, Constantine ordered his soldiers to demolish every altar of sacrifice to every god and quell any resistance. He then ordered the building of several large, centralised gathering places for his new religion. These multifunctional buildings, called 'basilicas', would also be used as courthouses, council chambers, and public meeting halls. They would inlcude an elevated area for the throne of the Emperor/Caesar/Pontiff to publicly wield his power in those three individual areas of his authority.

With this solution, religious practice could be brought under his direct control.

A Blood-Free Sacrifice: The desire to sacrifice was a major hindrance to Constantine's plans. The only religion that didn't need a blood sacrifice was the sect called The Way, as they believed the death of their Christ was the last sacrifice needed. He would now use that belief as the central theme of his new religion, with a ritualised performance of that last sacrifice at every gathering. Such action would engage the Christ-followers and, at the same time, appease the sacrifice-lovers. He would call these new gatherings *'the sacrifice of the mass'*. As 'mass' meant a large number of people without any particular belief system, this new title would be commonly understood to mean 'the official sacrifice for the general population'.

With this solution, people could participate in sacrifice without blood-letting.

Familiar Icons: To establish a successful combination of all religions into a new unified religion, Constantine incorporated familiar icons from various pagan ideologies. For example, the imgre of a goddess mother and god/child had been a common theme for centuries. This image was seen as Isis and son Horus in Egypt, Aphrodite and son Eros in Greece, Freya and son Baldur in Scandinavia, Yashoda and son Krishna in India, and Ashtoreth, Queen of Heaven and god/child Tammuz in Babylon. Thus, this familiar imagery was transformed by Constantine into the iconic image of the Virgin Mary and her god/child and included in his new one-world religion.

With this solution, multiple familiar pagan gods could be incorporated.

A Familiar Day Of Worship: It was important that the day set aside for the *'sacrifice of the mass'* would also be familiar and recognisable to the majority of Romans. Constantine worshipped the Greco-Roman sun gods, Sol, Zeus and Apollo. For him, 'Sun' day was 'the venerable day of the sun', the day he worshipped the sun god Sol. Thus, Constantine incorporated Sunday worship into his new religion. Prior to this, followers of The Way had observed the Jewish Sabbath as their holy day of rest, which began at sundown on Friday night and continued until sundown on Saturday night.

With this solution, Roman gods could be exalted and openly venerated.

Familiar Festivals: Constantine also celebrated the 'The Birthday of the Sun' (Sol), a long-practised pagan custom held annually during the winter solstice on the 25th of December, using lights as symbols of worship of Sol as the source of light. It was easy to incorporate this festival of rejoicing into his new religion. Calling it 'Christ for the masses', or Christmas, sold it as a Christian event, though it celebrated the birthday of a pagan god, not Christ.

With this solution, pagan celebrations could still be practised.

Creating A New Name: This sparkling new conglomeration of beliefs was Constantine's baby, and its main character needed a name. It would have to be one that all religions could accept, and a Hebrew name would not be acceptable. Thankfully, the Hebrew word 'Messiah' was easily translated into the Greek word 'Christ', so that was not a problem; however, there was the issue of the identifying name. Christ's name in Hebrew was Yahoshua, and its short form was Y'shua. This is the same name translated as Joshua everywhere else in Scripture, but it was Hebrew. So, instead of being translated as Joshua, Y'shua was transcribed letter for letter into the Greek Iesous, then the Latin Iesus, which later became the English Jesus. The phonetic result of this new name was a clever transformation of Y'shua into Y'zeus, a name Constantine could comfortably 'sell' to the pagans of Rome and logically explain to the faithful followers of Christ as a mere translation.

In changing our Saviour's name, Constantine totally undermined the concept of 'going' in Christ's name to fulfil the Great Commission.

In Hebrew, the name of Christ, Yahoshua Ha Messiah, means, *'God who is Salvation, The Anointed One'*. These two parts of Christ's name are inseparable; they show us who he is and how to go in his name. His full name reminds us that salvation comes through repentance, and signs and wonders come through his anointing. Those two parts of his name also show us how to obey Christ's Two Commandments because the Blood of the Lamb reveals we have loved God by repenting, and our testimonies reveal we have loved our neighbour.

We don't just 'go in his name', we live in his name, we overcome in his name, and we fulfil all his Commandments in his name. His name is everything, and Constantine flippantly changed it!

He knew what he was doing!

The previously unheard-of name, Jesus Christ, became the centre of Constantine's new State-controlled religion. History clearly shows that Constantine ordered Christ's new name because the famous Nicene Creed, established in 325AD under Constantine's rule, and still used in the *'sacrifice of the mass'* today, incorporated that new name.

With this solution, the worship of a totally new god could be controlled.

Creating The Doctrine: After establishing his new religion, Constantine ordered the confiscation and burning of all Apostolic writings and Hebrew Scriptures, making possession of them illegal. Anyone found in possession of such literature was put to death. This regulation of doctrine gave him control over what would be taught in his new religion. From then on, only official clergy were allowed to present and explain accepted Scripture. This destroyed the freedom of all believers, men, women, and children, to gather together to read from the known word, share testimonies, bring a spiritual message, sing whatever song was on their heart, or share a recent revelation of truth. These things were now illegal.

> With this solution, doctrine could be overseen by the State.

Controlling His Clergy: As Pontiff, Constantine had absolute power to grant lordly 'privileges' to the most loyal of his new clergy class. He established them as 'overlords' and authorised them to keep adherents subservient to his new religion. The most successful low-level clergy were rewarded with land and offered promotion to higher office. Higher office meant political power and wealth. In doing this, Constantine obliterated the concept of leaders as servants who 'wait on the tables' of those who go out into the world to do the work of ministry.

> With this solution, clergy could be controlled by the State.

But he still wasn't finished!

Using His New Religion Against Christ: The final abomination came after the loyal followers of The Way began calling for a return to obedient service to Christ and his Great Commission. Constantine did not call these faithful believers Christians but named them Donatists after their leader, Donatus Magnus.

The Donatists asserted that leadership should not be administered by 'traditores' (from the same root word as 'traitor' and 'tradition') who gained clergy positions in the new religion after handing over Apostolic teachings to be burned or by exposing those who were keeping them hidden. They claimed that the traditores were betraying their Messiah and his saints in order to promote themselves.

Constantine assembled an army against the Donatists. Not Roman soldiers this time, but zealous adherents of his new religion. To prove their allegiance to their new religion, they squashed the Donatist uprising, killing many believers. The remnant of Christ's faithful could only save themselves by fleeing to Africa, far from Constantine's control.

This was the first time in history that those who called themselves followers of Christ, or Christians, traded pacifism for brutality, becoming violent and willing persecutors of the true followers of Christ.

The establishment of the new counterfeit Christianity was now complete!

A successful hijack!

Constantine had crushed the sect known as The Way and corralled it, along with all but one of the other religions of the known world, into his new, one-size-fits-all, universal State-run religion. He was a success! The problem of religion was solved!

Soon after, Constantine gained the accolades he desired. His religious strategy was widely regarded as politically brilliant. He became so famous throughout the Roman Empire for his ability to effectively combine various belief systems and stop the problem of religious disharmony that he was hailed as Constantine the Great.

Constantine's politically shrewd universal religion became known as the Roman Catholic Church. Since 'Catholic' means 'universal,' this was the perfect clinical name for a cold and clinical resolution to a highly emotional problem. Over the next 1000 years, his new emotionless religious structure became firmly established and hailed as the only true and acceptable religion for the civilised world.

One religion refused to join!

The Jews rejected this abomination outright, and their rejection began an avalanche of targeted persecution of Jews throughout Europe. Adherents of the new religion were told that Jews killed their Saviour, and so a tidal wave of hatred of Jews began. Antisemitism was born!

The Jews didn't kill Christ; they asked for him to be killed, but it was the Romans who killed him. Roman soldiers didn't just kill him; they gleefully tortured him before subjecting him to the cruellest possible death. The unnecessary cruelty of his torture and death at the hands of Roman soldiers is glorified in the 'Stations of the Cross', which line the walls of almost every Roman Catholic church.

The same people who killed him, later venerated him and blamed the Jews for his death. Yet the truth remains. Christ's torture and death were ordered under the authority of the second Emperor/Caesar/Pope of Rome, Tiberius. History records that despite publicly declaring Christ innocent of any wrongdoing, Roman Governor Pontius Pilate ordered his death.

But who would know the truth? Catholics were not allowed to read Scripture. They only knew what the clergy told them. And the clergy only told the people what the Pope/Emperor/Caesar wanted them to know. Catholics had no clue that hatred of Jews was a result of their founding Pope's vendetta against those who had rejected his decree.

This lie is still in effect!

This notorious lie was the reason for the famous Massacre of Jews by Catholics in Spain in 1931, later becoming one of the accepted excuses for the genocide of around six million Jews during the Nazi holocaust. Even today, people do not associate the death of Christ with Rome. But how can they not?

Powerful propaganda!

Another absurd lie given to legitimise Catholicism as the 'true church' or 'original Way of Christ' was that Peter was the first Pope. This is impossible as Peter was not a Roman, and more importantly, he was never Emperor of Rome, or Caesar.

A well-known alternative title to Emperor is Caesar, but a less well-known title is *'Pontifex Maximus'*, meaning chief high priest of religion or Pontiff. Even today, the Pope retains this triple title. No Pope can hold the title of *Pontifex Maximus* without simultaneously holding the other Imperial titles, *Emperor* and *Caesar*.

This is why the Pope has always been regarded as infallible and why people are expected to greet him by bowing in submission and kissing his ring. He is the continuing deified Emperor and all-powerful Caesar of Rome! Why hide this truth?

The first Pope/Emperor/Caesar of Rome was Augustus Caesar, who ordered the census that took Mary and Joseph to Bethlehem.

The second Pope/Emperor/Caesar of Rome was Tiberius Caesar, under whose authority Christ was tortured and put to death.

Then followed Caligula, Nero, Diocletian and fifty other notorious Popes of Rome, whose atrocities were so great that most were killed by their family members or trusted soldiers.

By the time Pope Constantine came along, the life expectancy for a serving Emperor/Caesar/Pope was very short. So, in this regard, his decision to support his soldiers was a matter of self-preservation.

He did not follow Christ!

Though he created the pseudo-Christianity initially known as Catholicism and was regarded as the first Christian Emperor, he actively persecuted followers of The Way, heavily fined every Roman citizen who didn't become a Catholic and withheld promotions from those in high office who would not convert.

Hypocritically, he personally remained a pagan all his life, communicating with Apollo, depicting the image of Sol on his shield and imprinting it on Imperial coins. Though it is claimed he was baptised into his own religion while on his deathbed, that is debated, and that he was baptised at all is disputed.

The reality is that Constantine was never a follower of Christ, and what he did to The Way of Christ is an abomination. His legacy is the desolation he brought to the precious and powerful name of Christ, to Christ's great and effective Commission, to the joyful sharing of testimony at every gathering of believers, and to servant-heart leadership. He founded a cult-like program of pseudo-religion and filled it with leaders whose purpose was to 'lord' it over others to protect or enhance their own lives.

He trampled true worship!

When you see
standing in the holy place
'the abomination that
causes desolation'
spoken of by Daniel,
flee to the mountains.

- Matt. 24:15-16 -

Breaking the chains!

CHAPTER 3

The
unparalleled power,
and
effectiveness of
Christ's
way of worship!

LIVING SACRIFICES

Satan's greatest weapon against The Way of Christ was the trampling of the true worship that Christ himself taught through example. It was Christ's worship of his Father through the cross that broke the power of Satan's reign on earth, forever! There is nothing more powerful than Christ's way of worship!

After his resurrection and the coming of his promised Spirit at Pentecost, Christ's way of worship empowered the spread of the Gospel and encouraged the first disciples and centuries of generational disciples to stand firm as they faced various hate-filled persecutions. Obviously, this kind of worship was too powerful and had to go! So, Constantine shut it down!

> *His forces will rise up and desecrate the temple fortress. They will abolish the daily sacrifice and set up the abomination of desolation. Daniel 11:31*
>
> *It will prosper in everything it does, and truth will be thrown to the ground. Daniel 8:12*
>
> *With flattery, he will corrupt those who violate the covenant, but the people who know their God will firmly resist him. Daniel 11:32*

The purpose of the abomination prophesied by Daniel was to '*abolish the daily sacrifice*' and '*throw truth to the ground*'. That is what Satan did to Christ through his arrest, torture and execution, and also what Constantine later continued to do to Christ's faithful followers.

Despite pretenders in the churches today who push the fantastical psy-fi illusion that Daniel's prophesied abomination hasn't happened yet, but will supposedly usher in a future Satanic antichrist figure who will destroy the world with his despotic and chaotic one world government, the actual prophesy of Daniel was thoroughly fulfilled over 2000 years ago, as can plainly be seen.

- The orders for the arrest of Christ came from the highest temple authority ruling over God's people. Those orders were an abomination.

- The temple those orders came from, where true worship, the truth himself, was *'thrown to the ground'*, was the already rebuilt temple in Jerusalem.

- Further, it was only because Rome ruled over the Holy Land that Christ could fulfil Scripture by dying on a cross, for crucifixion was an extreme torture made famous by the Roman Empire.

Those three totally separate but combined circumstances (ruler in the temple, rebuilt temple, Roman Empire) thoroughly fulfilled the prophecy of Daniel in Christ's time.

It was clearly the religious abomination ruling in God's rebuilt temple in Jerusalem, under Roman authority, who *'threw truth to the ground'* and stopped Christ's own *'daily sacrifice'* of worship by handing Christ over to be put to death.

Likewise, it is easy to see that Constantine stopped the daily sacrifice of Christ's followers, which was the source of their strength. He deliberately substituted their extended daily gatherings with one hour on Sundays, replaced shared meals of remembrance with a token communion, and supplanted the free sharing of testimony, revelations and Scripture with monologues from men in pulpits.

The true meaning of worship was ignored completely, and the word 'worship' watered down. It quickly became just another word for gathering together for a short '*sacrifice of the mass*' on Sundays, or a general description for the singing of praises to God. Yet worship is neither of these things, and our *daily sacrifice* is still of paramount importance to God.

Exceedingly powerful!

> *I urge you, brothers and sisters, in view of God's mercy, to offer your bodies as a living sacrifice, holy and pleasing to God. This is your true and proper worship. Romans 12:1*

It is in understanding that God wants us to *offer our bodies as a living sacrifice* to Him daily, and that He regards our total submission to Him each day as our only *holy and pleasing worship,* that we begin to realise that what we have been told about worship is simply not true. Furthermore, it becomes important for us to personally understand what God means by '*living sacrifice*'.

What is a living sacrifice?

The power hidden in Christ's sacrifice on the cross is extraordinary. Christ didn't just offer himself up to die. Everyone dies. No one can avoid dying. But before he died, Christ presented himself to his Father as *a living sacrifice*, and this is what made the difference. This act of submission was pure worship, and it is this kind of worship that God converts into powerful spiritual warfare.

Before Christ was arrested, he implored his Father to release him from the coming agony. His prayer was so intense that he sweated blood. Nevertheless, God did not release him. Christ's response at that point made him *a living sacrifice*. He was completely submitted to the will of his loving Father.

Father, if You are willing, take this cup from Me. Yet not My will, but Yours be done. Luke 22:41-47

Prior to this prayer, Christ had presented his whole life to God, body, soul and spirit. We know that he occasionally attended the temple, that he sang songs of praise with his disciples when they shared meals, and that he often went off alone to pray. But he also publicly obeyed his Father's will, healed the sick, raised the dead, cast out demons and preached the Gospel of Repentance wherever he went. All this was done in submission to the general will of God.

But the cross was different!

For our struggle is not against flesh and blood, but against unseen rulers and authorities, against the cosmic powers of this world's darkness, and against the spiritual forces of evil in the heavenly realms. Ephesians 6:12

All the dark cosmic powers and spiritual forces Satan had previously employed to deceive, trick, trap, confuse and destroy God's children were overcome on the cross simply because Christ understood the power of becoming *a living sacrifice.*

Worship breaks chains!

When Christ chose to go to the cross as *a living sacrifice*, it was not only the most loving expression of worship that will ever be seen in heaven or on earth, but it was also the most powerful execution of spiritual warfare that mankind will ever know.

Simultaneously passive toward God and aggressive toward Satan, Christ's death reveals that our worship, like his, will always automatically sabotage Satan's plans.

While he was on the cross, Christ demonstrated five spiritual aspects to being a *living sacrifice* that worked together to obliterate the power of Satan. Individually, they are powerful, for they show us five different ways to present our bodies to God as *living sacrifices*. But when used together, these five become powerful weapons that break all Satanic chains. Satan can't fight them! They are beyond his reach and therefore beyond his power!

Repentance, Testimony, Love, Prayer and Submission to God's will were the five aspects of Christ's living sacrifice that, when used together, broke the power of Satan's authority, forever.

When we use these five not-so-ordinary tools in the same way Christ used them, they become for us an invincible weapon of spiritual warfare that literally shatters the forces of darkness.

Greater authority than angels!

Hallelujah! Praise the Lord in the heavens, praise him in the highest places. Praise him, all his angels! Praise him all the armies of heaven! Psalm 148:1-2

From the time Constantine watered down the power of worship, singing praises has been referred to as worship; however, worship from the redeemed has a higher function than praise. Angels can sing praise, but they can't present themselves to God as *a living sacrifice*. This pure spiritual worship puts us, with Christ, in a position higher than God's angels can attain. In that high position, Satan and his army of rebel angels cannot touch us. We are out of their reach and beyond their power.

This does not mean we should not sing praise, for during times of corporate praise when we sing songs of adoration, otherwise ordinary humans can often feel the presence of God. It's like we have entered heaven and are singing with the angels at the foot of his throne.

You are holy, Oh Lord, enthroned on the praises of your people. Psalm 22:3

Not understanding that worship is more than praise, Constantine sought to control the emotion of personal adoration by introducing choirs. Our personal responsibility to sing praise to God was delegated to others, and so the presence of God, which used to be so often felt in praise, disappeared.

Though Constantine deliberately tried to control, every aspect of Christ's Way of worship, he failed, for he didn't understand that worship is more than praise. There is still nothing in heaven or earth can stop the chain-breaking effect of Christ's five-fold way of presenting his life to God as *a living sacrifice.*

Repentance breaks chains!

Constantine watered down repentance when he introduced the *'sacrament of confession'* administered only by paid clergy. This was a very clever 'big-brother' way for a government to spy on its people. 'Confession' changed the entire understanding of the purpose of repentance, which was never merely about confessing sin, but rather has always been the key to healing.

Is any one of you sick? He should call the elders of the church to pray over him and anoint him with oil in the name of the Lord.

The prayer in faith will restore the one who is sick. The Lord will raise him up. If he has sinned, he will be forgiven. James 5:14-15

> *Some men brought to him a paralysed man, lying on a mat. When Christ saw their faith, he said to the man, "Take heart, your sins are forgiven".*
>
> *On seeing this, some of the scribes said to themselves, "This man is blaspheming!"*
>
> *But Christ knew what they were thinking and said to them, "Which is easier: to say, 'Your sins are forgiven', or to say, 'Get up and walk'?" Matthew 9:2-4*

Confession is not repentance. Repentance has the power to break the chains of sickness over people's lives so much so that Christ referred to healing and forgiveness as interchangeable, or one and the same. If we can grasp it, this is an incredibly powerful concept.

The Apostle Paul describes repentance as the first thing we need to learn as we begin living as Christians. It is the foundation of everything a follower of Christ believes. Without this in place, no one can *go on to maturity* in Christ. Nothing else can be built.

> *Therefore, let us leave the elementary teachings about Christ and go on to maturity, not laying again the foundation of repentance from works that lead to death, and of faith in God. Hebrews 6:1*

Don't think for a moment that Constantine didn't know what followers of The Way believed. He carefully structured his shiny new religion to contain all the elements, but none of the power.

We overcome him (Satan) by the blood of the Lamb and the word of our Testimony. Revelation 12:14

Constantine deliberately attempted to dilute the power of repentance and its core purpose as the foundation of Christ's Way because the full might of the Roman Empire had not been able to quench this core belief. He knew repentance was the source of the authority, power, strength, and experience that allowed even children to do the miraculous.

Heal the sick, raise the dead, cleanse the lepers, drive out demons. Freely you have received; freely give. Matthew 10:8

Angels can't touch repentance!

Repentance is another area where angels have no authority. Angels can't repent of sin, can't be covered by the blood of Christ and can't be redeemed. When we step into repentance, no angel can follow us, for we step directly into the inner sanctum of God's holy power. In that place, sickness can't live, Christ's forgiveness can't be undone, and Satan can't touch us. We are out of his reach.

Repentance is a powerful chain-breaker and an unbeatable disease-shatterer. It is one of the smartest things anyone on this earth can do. And telling people about the power of repentance to set them free from all their sins and diseases is one of the greatest gifts we can give to anyone. 'Confession' is hollow in comparison!

Testimony breaks chains!

We overcome not just *by the blood of the Lamb* but also *by the word of our testimony, Revelation 12:14.* So what is so powerful about our testimony?

> *We believe man's testimony; but God's testimony is much stronger...whoever does not believe God, has made a liar of Him, because he has not believed what God (the Spirit) has said about His Son. 1John 5:6-11*

It is not 'our' testimony that breaks chains, but the testimony of the Spirit of God given through us that breaks chains. His personal witness to the work of Christ through us is vital proof of the ongoing effectiveness of Christ's death and resurrection. The testimony we give may be ours, but it will only be valid in heavenly places if it is given by the Spirit of God living in us.

It is HIS witness that counts!

The Spirit of God is God's only true witness. It is His role to verify and promote the actions and works of both God and Christ. Therefore, every valid testimony given by the Spirit of God through us will always and only glorify God and Christ.

The testimony of the Spirit of God is the testimony of God Himself, for they are 'one'. If anyone, including Satan, does not believe the testimony given by the Spirit of God through us, they *'make God a liar'*. Not a smart thing to do!

Christ confirmed the necessity of the Spirit's witness when he made the remarkable statement that even his own self-testimony should not be regarded as valid.

> *If I testify on my own behalf, what I say is not to be accepted as proof. But there is one who testifies on my behalf, and I know what He says about me is true. John 5:31-32*

If 'self' testimony is invalid, then testimony must come from a source other than self. It must come from the Spirit of God. The valid testimony of the Spirit of God given through us will never glorify you, me or any other person; it will always and only glorify the work that Christ has already done.

> *There is one God and one mediator between God and men, Jesus Christ, who gave himself as a ransom for all men - the testimony given in its proper time. 1 Timothy 2:5-6*

When sharing our testimony, it is helpful to remember that true testimony is not about us or our denomination. The only testimony that will break chains and overcome the wiles of Satan is testimony about the work of Christ. We are the ransomed. We are the reason our Saviour died! The fact that Christ successfully ransomed us is *The Testimony*. It could stand alone on its own indisputable merits, yet incredibly, God has called us not only to witness what He has done but also personally testify to what Christ has done for us.

Angels can't give testimony!

As wonderful as God's holy angels are, they are merely God's servants. Although they praise God for His works day and night, they can never offer a personal testimony of redemption. They do not have a testimony, nor will they ever have a testimony. They have not been redeemed and therefore cannot glorify God for the saving work of Christ's blood in their lives.

They can never know the high privilege of having the Spirit of God dwell within them, for even though they live in the presence of God's Spirit, God's Spirit doesn't live in them. They are destined to remain servants and can never be regarded as sons or daughters of God. They will never share the role of Bride. They will never have a place beside Christ on his throne.

Though praise is something God expects from all his creation, testimony is privy only to those who know the saving power of the death and resurrection of His Son.

How privileged we are to be elevated above the angels! How privileged we are to have the opportunity to be witnesses to the saving work of Christ! How privileged we are to be invited by God Himself to tell others about this amazing arrangement. How privileged we are to be invited to share the eternal glory of Christ, simply because we now have His glorious Spirit living within us.

Eternal ramifications!

If this were the sum total of the role of testimony in the life of every believer, it would be enough, but our testimonies have far-reaching power.

Most believers are aware that *God dwells in the praises of His people, Psalm 22:3,* but only some know that His throne sits inside what is called the *'tabernacle of testimony'.*

> *After this, I looked, and the temple—the tabernacle of the Testimony—was opened in heaven. Revelation 15:5*

It is amazing to know that our praise is the throne on which God sits, and it's almost incomprehensible to realise that our testimonies to Christ make up the tabernacle surrounding His throne. But it becomes mind-blowing when we know that all the judgments of God written in the Book of Revelation come out from the Tabernacle of Testimony.

> *Out of the Tabernacle of Testimony came the seven angels with the seven plagues. They were given seven golden bowls full of the wrath of God. Revelation 15:6-7*

On the day of judgment, God will use the Spirit-empowered prayers and testimonies of his saints to bring about the final destruction of Satan and all who follow him. Every testimony we give is destined to be converted by God into burning coals of judgment.

Spiritual warfare does not get any more powerful than this!

Prayer breaks chains!

It is written, "My house shall be called a house of prayer for all generations". Matthew 21:13

The throne where God sits to receive praise is inside His *Tabernacle of Testimony,* yet Christ described God's dwelling place, or home, as *a house of prayer.*

These two descriptions are not at all contradictory because prayer is the source and the beginning of every testimony. Prayer will always increase Christ's testimony because the end result of faith-filled prayer is always more testimony.

This is where we begin to see the incredible, chain-busting power of prayer.

The key to praying prayers that God will convert to testimony is faith. Faith is not what we believe; it is what we do about what we believe. Faith is action! Our actions of faith are the evidence of our belief. We can pray all day and not get any results, but when we pray in faith, we will see results every time!

Faith is the substance of things hoped for, the evidence of things not seen. Hebrews 11:1

Prayer comes from hope. Hope is the sure and firm belief we hold in our hearts. Prayer is how we speak out the hope we hold in our hearts. But faith is the physical action we take to show we actually believe what we are praying for will happen.

Testimony comes from action!

The Scriptures tell us King David was *'a man after God's own heart'*, *1 Samuel 13:14.* That means he knew how to reach the heart of God in prayer. In the following story taken from 2 Samuel 15:3-34, King David teaches us how to pray in faith.

King David was in a spot of trouble. His son Absalom had usurped his kingship and was attempting to take David's kingdom by force.

David had two extremely wise, prophet-like, tactical advisers, Ahithophel and Hushai. They were respected by David and Absalom alike, yet amazingly, Ahithophel had decided to join with Absalom against God's anointed King.

When King David heard Ahithophel had joined Absalom's rebellion, he knew his ex-advisor's God-given wisdom would give his son a degree of success, so he prayed earnestly, *"Please, Lord, turn Ahithophel's advice into nonsense!"*

David's prayer was based on the confident assurance that God would uphold his position as anointed King and not allow anyone, including his son, to usurp his kingship. He was equally sure that God would not allow an anointed prophet to rebel against his kingship. He knew without a doubt that he was praying in line with God's will for his life. He was certain God would answer his prayer because he knew the character of God, but he didn't rest on prayer alone. After he prayed, he acted in faith.

David turned to his other trusted adviser, Hushai, and said, *"You can help me by returning to the city and telling Absalom you will now serve him as faithfully as you served his father. And then do all you can to oppose the advice that Ahithophel gives"*.

Hushai did as King David asked, joined Absalom's rebellion and ultimately found the opportunity to overturn Ahithophel's advice. God gave Hushai the needed wisdom to outsmart Ahithophel, and so Absalom's plans to kill his father were thwarted. As a direct consequence, Absalom was killed (v18:14), and Ahithophel committed suicide (v17:23).

King David didn't rely on prayer alone. Though he believed God would answer his prayer, he still applied an action of faith. As soon as he stepped out in faith, God showed up and brought the victory.

This is an unchanging principle!

Chain-breaking prayer will always include physical actions of faith that enable God to bring about the miracle we seek. And the resultant miracle will always become our testimony.

The more we pray in faith, the more miracles of answered prayer we will receive. The more answered prayers we receive, the more the testimony to Christ is increased on the earth and stored in heaven. This is the key to incredibly powerful, chain-breaking answered prayer.

Selfless love breaks chains!

I pray they all may be one as you Father are in me and I am in you, I pray they all may be one in us. That the world may believe that you have sent me. John 17:18-21

When I read the beautiful prayer Christ prayed on the night he was betrayed, I see nothing but his wholesome ambition to see God's children loving their heavenly Father the way he himself loved Him.

This prayer reveals that Christ's greatest hope is for us to be one with our eternal Father, and the reason for this hope is plainly stated, *so that the world may believe that God sent him.*

The world will not believe that God loves us and has sent His beloved Son into the world to reveal the Father's love, without obvious unity and oneness with God being shown by the redeemed.

This unity has nothing to do with people getting along with each other. The unity Christ is praying for is oneness with God through complete submission to his will. He wants all the redeemed to have the same relationship with his Father that he displayed.

It is amazing to know that the moment he finished praying this prayer, he completed it with an action of faith. His determination to remain one with God's will in Gethsemane, despite the excruciating pain it would bring, was the action of faith necessary to see victory on the cross.

Submission shows obedience!

Christ demonstrated unity and oneness with His Father through uncompromising obedience to His will. This is what he is asking us to do as well: show our love for him and God by obeying him, no matter how difficult obedience may become.

> *Anyone who loves me will obey my teaching. And my Father will love them and we will come to them and make our home with them.*
>
> *Anyone who does not love me will not obey my teaching. These words that you hear are not my own but belong to the Father who sent me. John 14:23-24*

This call to submit ourselves completely to God and Christ is mandatory for every believer. This is what it means to *take up our cross and follow him*. Although Constantine established a clergy class to relieve believers of the responsibility to take up our cross, this prayer of Christ still applies to every believer. Moreover, it applies to everyone who believes in Christ because of our message.

> *As you have sent me into the world, so I am sending them into the world. John 17:18*

There are no exceptions to this sending. Young, old, male, female, rich, poor, credentialed or not, every follower of Christ is called to step into unity with God and reveal his love to the world through noticeable obedience to Christ's Commandments and submission to God's will. This is love.

> *This is how we know that we love our fellow believers: by loving God and carrying out His Commands. In fact, this is love for God; that we keep His Commandments. 1John 5:2-3*

Loving God means keeping His commandments. Loving our neighbours and fellow believers means keeping His commandments. Submitting to His will means keeping His commandments. Living in unity and oneness with God means keeping His commandments. Submissive obedience to God's commandments is how we show the world His love.

Obedience shows love!

Living in submissive love, with God's commands central to everything we do, is what it means to present our bodies as *a living sacrifice*. Sometimes, keeping His commands will be a joy, like seeing someone turn from sin and become new in Christ, or witnessing a miracle. However, there will be times when submitting to God will clash with our own will, and those are the times when our *living sacrifice*, like Christ's, will become powerful spiritual warfare.

The first disciples and their disciples did not want to face the cruel pain of persecution or even death, but they overcame their fears by showing perfect love for God, as Christ did, through submission to God's will. That is perfect love. That is worship.

> *There is no fear in love, but perfect love drives out fear. The one who fears has not been perfected in love. 1 John 4:18*

These five overwhelmingly powerful aspects of true spiritual worship, Repentance, Testimony, Prayer, Love and complete Submission to God's will, when combined, destroyed Satan's power at Calvary and were the unstoppable driving force behind the rapid growth of Christ's Way for the first few centuries after he died, rose and sent his Spirit at Pentecost. They still can't be stopped!

Constantine needed to look beyond persecution to find another means of halting the five-fold power of *a living sacrifice* lifestyle. He chose misinformation and disinformation. He deleted Christ's God-given name and replaced it with one the pagan community could accept. He took commonly understood spiritual words and altered their meanings. He disguised ancient religious practices and presented them as new ideology. He watered down God's commands until they became unrecognisable.

Even today, many Christians still believe *worship* is about singing, *repentance* is about confessing sin, *testimony* is about personal victories, *praying in faith* is about believing God hears our prayers and *loving your neighbour* is about being nice to people. Wow! Not even close!

Constantine's deceptions were so successful that dictators today still use his methods to control their populations. Yet nothing can change the fact that the fake 'Christianity' he set up is no more than empty religion, while following Christ remains a lifestyle of loving submission. A daily living sacrifice.

Offer your bodies
as living sacrifices,
holy and pleasing to God,
which is your
spiritual worship.

- Romans 12:1 -

Ministry or control?

CHAPTER 4

Are
the redeemed
kings and priests
or mere
subordinates?

A NEW CLERGY CLASS

The Apostle Peter wrote the following after Christ specifically charged him with building a church that would follow Christ's Way. Far from being the first Pope or Bishop of Rome, Peter completely dismissed the role of priests as separate from the rest of us, explaining that we were now all part of *a royal priesthood* that belonged to *a holy nation*.

> *You are a chosen people, a royal priesthood, a holy nation, a people for God's own possession, to proclaim the virtues of Him who called you out of darkness into His marvellous light. 1 Peter 2:9*

The assurance this role gave believers helped them present their bodies to God as living sacrifices and accounted for the rapid increase of The Way. For over 275 years, despite heavy persecution, The Way of Christ grew and flourished in the hands of men, women and children who understood their role in *the priesthood of all believers*. Their loyalty was not to their earthly nation, but to the eternal Kingdom of God and the redeemed who were part of God's holy nation on earth.

Constantine wanted to stop this!

Constantine's solution to the problem of a virally spreading Gospel was to take the right to share the message of Christ out of the hands of ordinary men, women and children and make it the sole domain of paid clergy.

By creating a clergy class, he could restrict the spread of the Gospel and dampen the notion that all followers of Christ were *royal priests*. More importantly, he could annihilate the dangerous idea that, as *royal priests*, followers of The Way were a *holy nation*. To him, that notion was treason!

Trampling the covenant!

To the followers of The Way watching all these changes, this particular action by Constantine was *trampling the Son of God underfoot*, Hebrews 10:29. They were witnessing the corruption of Christ's holy covenant and the destruction of the costly freedom Christ had died to bring to mankind.

Creating a kingdom of priests for his God was the core purpose of the death and resurrection of Christ. Making God's children kings and priests to serve Him was the very thing that enabled Christ to endure the cross and later receive his title of King of Kings after he was raised from the dead.

> *You are worthy to take the scroll, and to open its seals. For you were slain, and have redeemed us to God by your blood. Out of every tribe and tongue and people and nation, and have made us kings and priests to our God. And we shall reign on the earth.* Revelation 5:9-10

Saving us to bring us into this position was the pivotal intention of the cross, and God delighted in Christ's victory by personally placing His royal seal on each and every one of Christ's precious redeemed.

God's Royal Seal!

In Him, you also, when you had heard the word of Truth, the Gospel of your salvation, and believed in Christ, were marked with the seal of the promised Holy Spirit. Ephesians 1:13

God's royal seal is His personal assurance that we belong to the Kingdom of Heaven. All hope of attaining eternal life is tied to understanding that it is the Spirit of God living in us that does the work of ministry. This truth has been buried so deeply that most who call themselves Christian today don't even know that the 'mark', or evidence, of the Spirit of God working through our lives is our guarantee of eternal life, *2 Corinthians 1:22.* Conversely, this means that without the Spirit doing Christ's work through us, we have no hope of eternal life.

The abomination strikes again!

Constantine trampled God's royal seal, the power of the cross, Christ's commission, God's commandments and the work of God's own Spirit under his feet. He showed nothing but contempt for God's plan for humanity, tossed God's plan to the ground, and elevated his own plan in its place.

These actions showed pure rebellion against God. In trampling the plan of God, the testimony of Christ, and the work of the Spirit under his feet, Constantine did what the *abomination of desolation* was designed to do: he used flattery to *throw truth to the ground* and *abolish the daily sacrifice.*

Nothing was left to chance!

In his State-controlled one-world religion, it wasn't enough for Constantine to deliberately introduce a clergy class that would destroy the freedom of Christ's followers to bring a spiritual message, sing whatever song was on their hearts, share a recent revelation of truth, proclaim a prophetic word or share testimony around a table as they broke bread and remembered Christ. No!

It wasn't enough for him to give Christ an 'acceptable' Romanesque name, repackage worship and corral it within a building for one hour per week, control praise with choirs, replace repentance with 'big brother' style confession, introduce conciliatory idol worship, and an enforced tax under the guise of giving. No! No! No!

More than all that, he couldn't stand the concept of this *royal priesthood*. After all, he was the Emperor/Caesar/Pontiff. His word was infallible. He was a god! He was the only 'royal priest' in his Empire. People submitted to him, knelt before him, kissed his ring, begged for his mercy. He held the power of life and death in his hands. He would never allow any other god to challenge his rightful national superiority. This royal priesthood had to go!

To the true followers of The Way, complying with the above was an outright betrayal of Christ. No wonder they called those who submitted to the new clergy 'traitors'. That's exactly what they were!

Despite what pretenders in pulpits still want us to believe so they can collect a 'tithe', Constantine's new clergy class was not based on the Hebrew priesthood, for in Messianic tradition, priests were not allowed to own property or receive a wage. This was unacceptable to Constantine.

His religion! His priests!

This new class of priests and bishops was an extension of Constantine's Imperial rule. Set up in the same manner as provincial and local governance, his new clergy class was no more than an extension of his political control. These new priests would serve Rome, not The Way of Christ.

His title, *Pontifex Maximus,* gave Constantine the legal authority to regulate and control all the priests in his Empire. To this end, he appointed several regional controllers and gave them the minor title 'Pontifex', meaning 'archpriests or bishops' who ruled over local priests.

And the new clergy class began!

Today, people argue that the role of 'bishop' was common even before Constantine, but that is impossible. As the word 'bishop' is derived from 'pontifex', the role of bishop could not exist outside Rome or without the approval of a ruling Emperor. Since Constantine was the only Roman Emperor ever to consider an alliance with the followers of The Way, the right to use 'pontifex' began with him.

Constantine was not finished!

I don't understand how anyone can believe that Constantine was a follower of Christ, because, to be honest, his actions show an absolute hatred of everything loved by God and Christ. Some of the things he did seemed to be petty, yet he did them anyway. One of the petty things he did was confuse the meaning of the word 'saint', which literally means 'set apart as holy to the Lord'.

Here is a call for the perseverance of the saints, who keep the commandments of God and the faith of Jesus. Revelation 14:12

In the early church, right up until the days of Constantine, the term 'saint' was interchangeable with 'believer'. It was what every follower of The Way was called. All believers were holy to the Lord.

Constantine altered the meaning of the word 'saint' to remove it from everyday use. He introduced various 'venerable saints' to be worshipped alongside Christ so that he could confine the word 'saint' to those considered superior to others. This was in line with Constantine's big-picture view of his new pseudo-religion, which included its members being called Christians, not saints.

Constantine was a genius at using words to manipulate. So much so that today, the Catholic Church still claims ownership of all 'saints' and only recognises as saints those whom they personally 'canonise' as worthy of the title.

Constantine tried everything he could to destroy the powerful testimony of Christ and recreate The Way of Christ in his own image. And his plan was politically effective! The State-controlled religion he set up is still in operation, and the membership name he created for followers of his purpose-built pseudo-religion is still called Christianity. Nevertheless, it can't be denied that the religion he founded does not resemble the freedom offered by Christ to the followers of His Way. Likewise, today, the lives of those known as Christians do not resemble the kinds of lives Christ and his disciples taught the saints of God to live.

It's not about religion!

Christ's commands, commission and spiritual truths cannot be adequately described as a religion. Rather, they are an all-embracing lifestyle where everything works together in harmonic unison.

- There is nothing more powerful in the Kingdom of God than true repentance through the blood of Christ, which brings salvation.
- There is nothing more powerful on earth than the signs and wonders that accompany salvation, providing testimonies to Christ's reality.

Together, Spirit-led Repentance and Testimony are the foundation stone of The Way of Christ. They are the solid rock on which Christ's church is built. They are the daily sacrifice for every believer and the prerequisite for being guaranteed eternal life.

A Way of living!

Personal repentance, through the blood of Christ, is how we fulfil Christ's First Commandment to *love God with our whole heart, soul, mind and strength*.

Openly keeping Christ's commandments and testifying to others about why we live Christ's Way is how we fulfil Christ's Second Commandment *to love our neighbour as ourselves.*

Living in repentance, actively testifying to the benefits of following Christ's Way and encouraging others to follow him with signs and wonders following, is how we fulfil Christ's Great Commission *to 'go' into all the world and make disciples, teaching them to obey everything I have commanded you.*

Christ's Way is crystal clear!

These commands are given to every man, woman and child who has been redeemed. Yet, they can only be obeyed by those who place themselves in partnership with the powerful Spirit of God. Without the Spirit of God, no one on earth can keep these Commandments of Christ.

This is what Constantine didn't understand. No human can contain, corral or claim ownership of the mighty Spirit of God. No human can stop the work of God's all-powerful Spirit. No religion can equal, replace or eclipse the unassailable supernatural work of God's mighty Spirit. Any attempted imitations will ultimately be seen as vapid, empty shells.

Who will listen
to me?
The word of the Lord
is offensive to them;
they find
no pleasure in it.

- Jeremiah 6:10 -

A monument to Rome!

CHAPTER 5

Saints,
bishops and
and implanted
history!

LEGACY OF LIES

All historical theories should be judged by logical merit. The logic of believing bishops existed before Constantine created the office of bishop defies logic. *Pontifex Maximus* (High Priest above all priests), also known as *Pontiff* (Pope), was a title given only to the Imperial Rulers of the Roman Empire. This title did not exist outside the Roman Empire.

The title *Pontifex Maximus* gave its holder the supreme authority to oversee all religious practices throughout the Roman Empire. Until Constantine, this authority had been widely used by most Pontiffs to persecute followers of The Way of Christ to death in the most vile and inhuman ways.

On the orders of the Emperor, Roman soldiers bore the burden of carrying out this inhumane killing, so it was no surprise that when they grew sick of killing people, the soldiers turned on their Emperor. This happened time and time again.

Constantine was the 55th Emperor since the first Emperor of the Roman Empire, Augustus Caesar, took power in 27BC. Mathematically, 55 Emperors over 333 years gives a mean rule of 6 years per Emperor. Not a promising outlook! Constantine was smart enough to read the mood of his soldiers. The killing would have to cease.

And so it did!

From the very beginning of his reign, Constantine saw finding a cure to the massive 'problem of religion' as his ticket to fame and glory. If he could find a solution to this ongoing problem, he would not only save his life but would be remembered as the first Emperor in history to come up with a viable solution. He would be known across the Empire as Constantine the Great.

He set to work!

Constantine was organised and knew how to rule. After choosing the only bloodless sacrifice system in the Empire to become the central *sacrifice of the mass* in his new religion, he commanded his soldiers to tear down every altar built for animal sacrifice. Then he commanded the building of four basilicas.

Designed to hold court hearings, council meetings, and religious gatherings, each rectangular basilica had a domed apse under which was a raised area for the Emperor, magistrate, or bishop to sit, and for priests to perform the *sacrifice of the mass* for the combined religious community. These buildings were a monument to the Roman Empire, not to Christ, and, like his new religion, highlighted the one-size-fits-all thinking of the Roman Empire.

Toward the end of his reign, after declaring Peter a 'Saint', Constantine ordered the building of St Peter's Basilica on the site where Peter was buried. Ironic that he was buried there because he was tortured and killed by Roman soldiers under Imperial order.

A hard sell!

In a multitheistic pagan society, abandoning belief in various purpose-oriented gods to serve just one God was a hard sell. So, the establishment of a new line of 'Christian' purpose-oriented saints seemed like the perfect solution. And it worked! Christianity became the most successful State-controlled religion the world has ever seen. Later, what he achieved was termed caesaropapism.

> *A secular, caesaropapist ruler is one who exercises supreme authority in ecclesiastic matters by virtue of his autonomous legitimacy. Max Weber (1864–1920)*

Everything Constantine did to establish his new religion was in keeping with the governance of the Roman Empire. This was his political solution to the massive problem of religion, and nothing would prevent him from being successful. He ordered his high officials to join his religion on pain of losing their status. He threatened to impose higher taxes on anyone in the Empire who refused to convert. And rewarded his newly appointed bishops and priests with tax breaks, social status and land holdings.

Appointing 'Venerable Saints' and sharing his title 'Pontifex' with his subordinates was entirely in line with his legitimate and supremely autonomous authority as Emperor/Caesar/Pontiff. Furthermore, it was his prerogative to present historical matters in a way that would not clash with his Imperial ambitions.

An example of this prerogative in action is seen after Constantine had his eldest son, Crispus, and his second wife, Empress Fausta, executed. After their deaths, he ordered every reference to them erased from literary records, historical records and inscriptions, so much so that neither is mentioned in his *Vita Constantini* (Life of Constantine the Great) written by Eusebius, who was appointed Bishop of Caesarea in 314, one of Constantine's first bishops and a person with no conscience about lying.

Tampering with history!

Taking data out of historical accounts and adding data into historical accounts are two sides of the same coin. If it was easy for Constantine to have people erased from history, how much easier was it for him to endow historically real people with titles they hadn't previously held—titles like 'Venerable Saint' or 'Bishop'? Doing so was his perogative!

The Apostle Peter was not known as Saint Peter before Constantine gave him that title. Nor was he ever Bishop of Rome until he posthumously received the title. What about the hundreds of other saints, posthumously given titles? Does it matter that most of the designated saints and bishops were killed by Roman Imperial order at the hands of Roman soldiers? Would they have been killed if they actually carried the Imperial authority of *Pontifex*? Paul's status as a Roman citizen made Roman soldiers hesitate to imprison him. They would certainly not have slaughtered someone with the high Roman title/rank of *Pontifex*.

What does Scripture tell us?

The word Pontifex (Latin:*Pontifex* translated *High Priest or Bishop*) is also (Greek:*archireús* translated *Archpriest or Bishop*). As most Scripture is written in Greek, the Greek word *archireús* is the one we look for in the following Scriptures.

> *A bishop (Greek:episkopon) then must be blameless, the husband of one wife, vigilant, sober, of good behaviour, given to hospitality, apt to teach. 1 Timothy 3:2*
>
> *For a bishop (Greek:episkopon) must be blameless, as the steward of God; not selfwilled, not soon angry, not given to wine, no striker, not given to filthy lucre. Titus 1:7*
>
> *If a man desire the office ('office' is not in the original text) of bishop (Greek:episkopēs) he desireth a good work. 1 Timothy 3:1*
>
> *For ye were as sheep going astray; but are now returned unto the Shepherd and Bishop (Greek:episkopon) of your souls. 1 Peter 2:25*
>
> *Paul and Timothy, bondservants of Jesus, To all the saints in Christ who are in Philippi, with the bishops (Greek:episkopois) and deacons (Greek:diakonois). Philippians 1:1*

These are the only five Biblical references to bishop or deacon in the early church, and all come from provable mistranslations in the King James version. No other version translates *episkopon, episkopēs* or *episkopois* as bishop, because these words don't mean bishop; they mean overseer, supervisor, or mentor. *Diakonois* means helper or assistant.

Although bishops, deacons, and venerable saints retroactively appeared in early church history after Constantine established these roles, neither the actual roles outlined in Scripture nor the teachings of the Apostles support them. The role of overseer, supervisor, or mentor was and still is entirely in line with the disciple-making role of every believer. While some saints were making disciples, some were being made disciples, and some were in between, assisting and helping. So, when Paul was writing these words, he was encouraging the saints who desired to make disciples to remember to practice what they preached. This is what he repeatedly taught and supported with his personal testimony.

> *I will not presume to speak of anything except what Christ has accomplished through me in leading the Gentiles to obedience by word and deed, by the power of signs and wonders, and by the power of the Spirit of God. So from Jerusalem all the way around to Illyricum, I have fully proclaimed the gospel of Christ. Romans 15:18-19*

Paul explained The Way

More than any other Apostle in the early church, Paul specified the roles believers could aspire to fill and explained how to fill those roles. There were many to choose from, and everyone was encouraged to follow the leading of God's Spirit. The most prominent of all Paul's teachings was that we should, at all costs, remain free to follow the Spirit of God and not revert to the legalism of religious works.

Christ gave some to be apostles, some to be prophets, some to be evangelists, and some to be pastors and teachers, to equip the saints for works of ministry and to build up the body of Christ. Ephesians 4:11-12

We have different gifts according to the grace given us. If one's gift is prophecy, let him use it in proportion to his faith; if it is serving, let him serve; if it is teaching, let him teach; if it is encouraging, let him encourage; if it is giving, let him give generously; if it is leading, let him lead with diligence; if it is showing mercy, let him do it cheerfully. Romans 12:6-8

There are different gifts, but the same Spirit. And different ministries, but the same Lord. There are different ways of working, but the same God works all things in all people. To each is given the manifestation of the Spirit for the common good. 1 Corinthians 12:4-7

Led by the Spirit!

It was for all the above reasons that leadership could not be confined to one role. The Spirit of God was in charge, and His leading was paramount. The various gifts and experiences within the entire body became the expertise within the body. It was called *the priesthood of all believers,* and this is The Way Christ intended His church to be built.

Peter said, "You are the Christ, the Son of the living God." Jesus replied, "This was not revealed to you by flesh and blood, but by my Father in heaven. And I tell you that on this rock I will build my church. Matthew 16:16-18

Peter agreed with Paul

The Apostle Peter, above all others, knew that Christ's church would be built on the 'rock' of individuals receiving guidance, revelation and power directly from the Spirit of God. He shared Paul's understanding of the multifaceted Way of Christ and encouraged every believer to present their lives to God and recognise His Spirit's leading in all they did.

> *Each of you should use whatever gift you have received to serve others, as faithful stewards of God's grace in its various forms. 1 Peter 4:10*

Along with Paul, Peter strongly warned the saints to guard against future false teachers who would introduce heretical teachings.

> *False teachers will come and secretly introduce destructive heresies, and because of them, The Way of truth will be defamed. 2 Peter 2:1-3*

> *Now the Spirit expressly states that some will abandon the faith to follow deceitful spirits and the teachings of demons, influenced by the hypocrisy of liars, whose consciences are seared with a hot iron. 1 Timothy 4:1-2*

Constantine used his political authority to do precisely what the first Apostles warned against. From the beginning, he deliberately designed a raft of heretical doctrines with the sole purpose of using The Way of Christ for personal gain. Worse, he used his political influence to rewrite church history to make it seem that his new religion was historically linked to Christ and therefore legitimate. It was not!

A structured system of priests under a hierarchy of bishops overseen by a Pope was as foreign to the Gospel of Christ then as it is now. Any priestly structure is still akin to the Old Mosaic Covenant, which Christ brought to an end. The first disciples, as one, regarded a return to such a system as a complete betrayal of Christ's sacrifice, and they warned against doing such a thing.

> *Anyone who rejected the law of Moses died without mercy on the testimony of two or three witnesses.*
>
> *How much more severely do you think someone deserves to be punished who has trampled the Son of God underfoot, treated as an unholy thing the blood of the covenant that sanctified them, and insulted the Spirit of grace? Hebrews 10:28-29*

The role of priests was to perform sacrifices to enable the forgiveness of sin. The New Covenant Christ ushered in did not require priests to stand in the gap between people and God because Christ broke down the barriers and became the only High Priest and intercessor we would ever need. Even today, genuine followers of Christ recognise no other high priest, bishop, reverend, minister or any other pastoral 'overlord' but Christ.

> *Unlike other high priests, Christ does not need to offer daily sacrifices. He sacrificed for sin once for all when he offered up himself. Hebrews 7:27*
>
> *God declared: "You are a priest forever in the order of Melchizedek." Hebrews 7:17*

One priest forever!

The new one-priest-forever system that Christ set up was the only priesthood structure the early disciples acknowledged. They went to their deaths rather than betray him. God had made Christ High Priest forever. No one could ever take his place.

> *Now, there have been many priests, since death prevented them from continuing in office. But because Jesus lives forever, He has a permanent priesthood. Hebrews 7:23-24*

Being part of *the priesthood of all believers* in service to our eternal High Priest did not involve holding an official office of any kind. This priesthood was a lifestyle of being individually led by the Spirit of God, day by day, as part of Christ's Kingdom.

Constantine was determined to wipe out *the priesthood of all believers*. To that end, he severely limited reading of Scripture, bringing revelation, proclaiming the message, laying on hands for healing, and sharing testimony. He changed the name of our Saviour, corralled worship within a building, controlled praise with choirs, replaced repentance with confession, added conciliatory idol worship, authorised 'Sun'day sacrifice and 'saint'hood, and successfully introduced a clergy class to run his new one-world religion. He had all but succeeded in destroying *the priesthood of all believers*. There was only one area left to conquer.

And he had a plan!

They worship me
in vain,
and teach as
doctrines
the precepts of men.

- Mark 7:7 -

A new tradition!

CHAPTER 6

The establishment of
'sacraments'
would place all things
into the hands
of the
new clergy class.

THE LORD'S TABLE

God changed everything. When Christ became our High Priest, it was because God changed the priesthood and all the ritual sacrifices that went with it, and He did that by changing the law. That is what the New Covenant is about. It is a change of law.

> *'When there is a change in the priesthood, the law must be changed as well. Hebrews 7:12*

Priesthood changes the law!

The New Covenant ushered in a new priesthood and the new punishment-free commandments could only come into effect because there was a change in the priesthood. Without a change in the priesthood there could not have been a change in the law.

The third and final change!

This New Covenant was the third change in God's order since Adam and Eve caused the fall. The first priesthood was set up by Adam to allow heads of families (Abel, Noah, Abraham) to offer sacrifices for forgiveness for the family. The second priesthood was set up by Moses to allow the Levites to offer sacrifices for forgiveness for the nation. This third and last priesthood was set up by Christ as the final sacrifice for forgiveness for all mankind.

> *Christ is the mediator of a new covenant, so that those who are called may receive the promised eternal inheritance. Hebrews 9:15*

A remarkable change!

In the previous two priesthoods, animals were offered for forgiveness of the various aspects of sin, both known and unknown, and sacrifices of grain and wine accompanied them as thanksgiving for the forgiveness received. This is how it worked.

- Mandatory: The *'Sin Offering'*, or *'Guilt Offering'*, was to atone for known sins.

- Mandatory: The *'Trespass Offering'* was to atone for sins committed unknowingly.

- Voluntary: The *'Burnt Offering'* was to cover sin in general, that is, to purify anything unclean by association.

- Voluntary: The *'Grain Offering'*, which also included wine, accompanied the burnt offerings and signified thanksgiving.

- Voluntary: The *'Peace Offering'* generally expressed peace and fellowship (repentance) between a person and God.

All the elements of every Adamic and Mosaic Old Testament sacrifice, both voluntary and mandatory, are listed above. A lamb could be used to atone for 'sin' or 'guilt', and a ram was used for 'trespass' offerings. A lamb could also be used for the 'burnt' offerings and as a 'peace' offering to God. The concept of these sacrifices didn't change with Christ, but the application did. He fulfilled them!

Both High Priest and Sacrifice!

As Lamb of God, Christ became our *sin, guilt,* and *trespass* offerings, covering both our known sins and unknown sins. As such, he fulfilled all the *mandatory* requirements of the Law regarding forgiveness for sin. Likewise, as the Lamb of God, his sacrifice also fulfilled the *voluntary* requirements of the Law in regard to the *burnt* offering for sin in general and the *peace* offering, which brought peace or favour with God. So, our High Priest, in dying in our place, legally became for us:

- the mandatory sin offering,
- the mandatory guilt offering,
- the mandatory trespass offering,
- the voluntary burnt offering, and
- the voluntary peace offering.

> *For he is our peace, who has made the two one and has torn down the dividing wall of hostility. Eph.2:14-16*

There was only one final, voluntary aspect of the old sacrifice system that God carried over into the New Covenant. The 'grain' offering.

The grain offering, which included wine, always signified thanksgiving to God for the forgiveness already received. It was not just an idea; it was law! Put in place by God, this law had been practised by his people for thousands of years, and the way it was practised was important to God, and still is!

> *Is not the cup of thanksgiving for which we give thanks a participation in the blood of Christ? And is not the bread we break a participation in the body of Christ? 1 Corinthians 10:16*

The Lord's Table was given to us by Christ so we could remember how he fulfilled the Law of God and ushered in a New Covenant written in his blood. He asked us to remember to give thanks to God for his overriding sacrifice and the forgiveness now available to everyone who believes in his atoning work. And, he told us precisely how it was to be done.

While they were eating...

Eating is central to life. Most people gather to eat at least once a day. Christ took this normal human activity and made it the focal theme for all fellowship in his new church. This is how his church would gather, around a meal in a home, but not just any meal. What Christ was about to do would turn every ordinary meal into a service of worship.

> *While they were eating, Jesus took bread and gave thanks, and broke it and gave it to his disciples saying, "Take, eat, this is my body." Then he took the cup, gave thanks and offered it to them saying, "Drink from it, all of you, this is my blood of the covenant, which is poured out for many for the forgiveness of sins." Matthew 26:26-27*

This concept was not new to the disciples. Celebrating forgiveness with a meal had been part of Jewish tradition for thousands of years.

Under the previous covenant, the 'bread and wine of thanksgiving' was shared only during special commemorative meals, such as the Passover. Under the new covenant, thanksgiving was to be shared at every meal. This was a huge difference, but the law was the same. The disciples of Christ faithfully, and with reverence for this long-standing law, passed Christ's Way along to all new disciples. At every mealtime gathering, they remembered Christ's great sacrifice, and so every meal became an opportunity to share all the good Christ was doing for them in an attitude of thanksgiving.

Led by the Spirit of God, multiple meal-based gatherings of believers sprang up like mushrooms and were the powerhouse of the first disciples and centuries of their disciples. Their joy-filled fellowship with God, Christ, the Spirit and other believers was the reason they could boldly embrace Christ's Commission and bravely face horrific persecution.

Constantine was determined to destroy these gatherings. They were the bane of his existence and the reason he needed to establish a new religion. He was determined to crush them. The last nail in the coffin of *the priesthood of all believers* was the corruption of The Lord's Table. Constantine's plan was to ritualise the breaking of bread and drinking of wine and include it in the *sacrifice of the mass* as a new 'sacrament' that could only be performed by priests. In keeping with the 'common religious union' he was promoting, he would call it *Communion*.

Constantine didn't understand the limits of his authority. He thought he could create his own brand of priesthood and attach it to God's New Covenant, but he couldn't. A covenant is a legal contract. God's new *High Priest* over a *priesthood of all believers* could never be removed from the New Covenant. Removing the priesthood would void the covenant.

In changing the 'priesthood', Constantine broke away from the contract God made with Christ. That left him with no access to the promised rewards of the New Covenant, including eternal life. Under his apostate priesthood, the Covenant set up between God and Christ became irrelevant and inaccessible to him and the converts to his pseudo-religion.

Terms of the Covenant

The terms of God's New Covenant with Christ were very clear. Christ would be the *High Priest* over a widespread *priesthood of all believers*. God's own Spirit would empower Christ's covenant priesthood to do the work of ministry in The Way demonstrated by Christ, their High Priest. Christ's legitimate priesthood, his redeemed men women and children, would heal the sick, cast out demons, speak in the language of angels, baptise new believers in water and the Spirit, teach new disciples to see God at work and work with him to do his will, overcome the forces of darkness and bring the Kingdom of Heaven to Earth every day. In return, all the Covenant rewards would be accessible to this *priesthood of believers*.

These rewards would not only be accessible, they would be exclusive to Christ's loyal *priesthood of believers*. People outside Christ's New Covenant priesthood would not be eligible to receive God's heavenly rewards. These rewards would include entry through gates of pearl in jewelled walls, to streets of gold, mansions, peace, safety and eternal bliss.

- No more tears or crying,
- No more death or mourning,
- No more pain or punishment,
- No more hunger or thirst,
- No more darkness, only light,
- Everything will be made new,
- Everything will be precious,
- Everything will shine with beauty.

> *It will shine with the glory of God, and its appearance will be like a very precious jewel, like jasper as clear as crystal...*
>
> *The city will be pure gold as clear as glass, and the foundations of the walls will be made of every kind of precious stone.*
>
> *Each of the twelve gates will be made out of a single pearl, and the street of the city will be pure gold. On no day will its gates ever be shut.*
>
> *The river of the water of life, clear as crystal, will come out from the Throne of God and of his Son. And there will be no more night, for the Lord God will give them continual light.*
>
> *Revelation.21:11,18,19,21 & 22:1-5*

One legitimate priesthood!

When Constantine shut down *the priesthood of all believers,* he shut down the only legal access God provided to the rewards of eternal life. He appropriated the concepts of Heaven and Hell from Christ and promised eternal life for submission to his new priesthood and new religion. But, Constantine didn't have the authority to promise eternal life to anyone for anything. Eternal life was not his to grant.

The New Covenant has not changed. Eternal life is still only available to those who meet the terms of the agreement made by God with Christ. Becoming part of Christ's *priesthood of all believers* is still the only Way to Heaven. Following the paid clergy system of denominational religion is not The Way and never will be. It is the greatest deception in history!

A sacred military oath!

Constantine appropriated all his ideas from others. Even the idea of 'sacraments' was stolen. The Latin term *sacrāmentum* (sacred oath) had been used in Ancient Rome as the oath of allegiance taken by soldiers as they pledged service to Rome above all else. Now, via these new 'sacraments', Constantine required a sacred oath of allegiance to his new Roman religion and those who didn't swear allegiance paid a heavy price. Later, that price was officially called in Greek *anathema* (offered up to be hated, shunned, excommunicated or cursed by God).

They claim to
know God,
but by their actions
they deny him.

- Titus 1:16 -

My personal journey!

CHAPTER 7

Removing the
priesthood
of all believers
from the
ogre
of religion.

THE ANATHEMA

The hand of God was clearly on my life before I was born, for he placed me into a family of contrasts. A place where love was abundant and hate was hidden, with no clear line of distinction between the two. On one side, there was obvious love, belonging and protection. On the other side, in shades of grey, there was rejection, shallow vanity and constant betrayal, wrapped in a cloak of respectability.

This was my training ground!

I am so grateful to God for my father, who taught me to question everything, to look beyond the accepted and embrace every problem as a creative challenge. He was warm, loving, intelligent, playful, inventive, protective and reliable. He taught his children, through demonstration, unusual things like how to survive in the Australian desert or where to go in Sydney's Blue Mountains to see water roll uphill. Over dinner, he would ask us to pass the NaCl (the chemical formula for table salt) or read Aristotle's opinions about young people. He made learning fun. My inheritance from him was an insatiable search for truth. He died when I was 23, and I still miss him every day.

My mother was his complete opposite. She didn't question anything, but rigidly conformed to the status quo. Change was the enemy, and education and creativity were to be endured rather than embraced.

She loved to dress smartly, party and entertain her friends, but had no ambition, didn't work, didn't like gardening, didn't like animals and didn't like her children. The only area of her life I could emulate was her hospitality.

My parents were as unequally yoked as any two people could be. Besides hospitality, their only common ground was the Catholic church. Nevertheless, *God works all things for good for those who love him and are called according to his purpose,* Romans 8:28.

Though I didn't know it when I was young, I was called according to God's purpose. He had deliberately placed me in this family. The mixture of love and respectable hate that I had been born into would become my most valuable life lesson.

> *Train up a child in the way he should go and when he is old he will not depart from it. Proverbs 22:6*

Looking back over the years, it is now easy for me to see that God himself chose my training ground in order to equip me with the skills I would need to do the job he had created me to do. The details of his planning still blow me away!

I was the second of six children in what was regarded as a normal family, as normal as any large Irish-Catholic family can be. Life was happy, easy, a colourful blur, until I was seven when my eyes suddenly opened and ambition was born.

One would expect the first ambition of a little girl to be something normal, like wanting to be a mother, or a nurse, or a ballerina, but no, my first ambition was really weird for a child, and through I didn't know it at the time, totally in line with the will of God for my life.

I wanted to rescue God's priests!

Seven is the age in the Catholic church when children are allowed to participate in Communion. My First Communion was special to me because I knew, even at such a young age, that I loved Christ and my desire to serve him was genuine. But that was not the eye-opener!

A few days after my First Communion, I was asked by my teacher, a nun, to take a small package over to the priest in the presbytery. It wasn't far away. The convent, school, church and presbytery were all on the same block of land, in that order, with no fences between them.

When I arrived at the presbytery, a grumpy old lady opened the door. She was probably only in her 40s, but to a seven-year-old, she looked ancient. *"What do you want?"* she growled, and I told her I had a parcel for the priest. "I'll give it to him," she said and reached down to take the package from me. I hesitated. I'd been told to give the parcel to the priest, and I was an obedient child, so handing it over to someone else felt like I was being made to be disobedient.

I looked past the woman to the priest, sitting alone in his office, eating a sandwich, and I suddenly felt very sorry for him. In my childish mind, he was like a prisoner being held captive by a cranky, old ogre. I wanted to set him free. But I was only seven. So, I offered up the parcel to the ogre and watched as she closed the door.

My ambition was born!

As I turned away to go back to the school, I determined that when I grew up, I would work in God's house and help the priests, but I would not be an ogre; I would be nice. I didn't know then about *the priesthood of all believers*; I wouldn't know about it for over a decade. I didn't know that embracing this first ambition was, in effect, my 'yes' to the call of God. And I didn't realise until much later that the encounter itself was like a parable of the shape my life was already beginning to take; seeking out God's royal priests, but being confronted instead by ogres, otherwise known as respectable wolves in sheep's clothing who accompany the royal priesthood like tares accompany wheat.

> I was only seven, but God was already directing my steps!

At ten years of age, I was baptised in the Spirit by the laying on of hands. The Catholic church calls it Confirmation, and despite my association with the apostasy of the Catholic religion, God accepted me as worthy and filled me with his glorious Spirit.

> *Do not neglect the spiritual gift that is in you, which was given you through prophecy when the body of elders laid their hands on you. 1 Timothy 4:14*

I didn't know what it meant to be filled with the Spirit, and so I didn't expect anything to change, but there was a change. I don't know when it happened, but over time, I noticed that I had developed a passionate desire to stand up for Christ. This desire would burst out of my heart every time I sang the words to *We Stand For God*. When I sang this hymn, I couldn't stand tall enough, I couldn't sing it loud enough, and I couldn't sing it often enough. I meant every word, and those words pounded in my heart and in my head and directed the focus of my worship and my understanding of service. The passion I felt when I sang that hymn showed me I loved Christ with all my heart and would be prepared to die for him if necessary.

WE STAND FOR GOD
(written by J.P. O'Daly in May 1940)

We stand for God and for his glory,
The Lord supreme and God of all;
Against his foes, we raise his standard;
Around the cross, we heed his call.
Strengthen our faith, Redeemer;
Guard us when danger is nigh;
To thee we pledge our lives and service,
For God we live, for God we'll die:
To thee we pledge our lives and service,
For God we live, for God we die.

My first assignment!

When I was fifteen, God gave me my first chance to confront a wolf in sheep's clothing. I didn't know then there were such things as wolves, and I'd never heard of false prophets. As you can expect, growing up, I was involved in everything Catholic, from the church choir to helping in the kitchen at retreats. I was also part of the weekly Catholic youth group run through our local parish. This group was quite large and made up of young people from both Catholic and non-Catholic backgrounds. Everything ran smoothly, everyone was happy, and there were no major issues. That is, until a brash young priest arrived in the parish and was immediately appointed leader over the youth.

Convert or leave!

The first thing this priest did was divide our group into Catholic and non-Catholic, and every week, he would explain why our Catholic group should not be contaminated with non-Catholics. Our group had been meeting for years, and we were all friends, so, as you can imagine, the assertion that those who were not Catholic did not belong to God or to our youth group caused a lot of pain and hurt. I didn't like what this priest was doing, and I wanted to stop him from hurting people, but I was only fifteen and I didn't know what to do. So, I confided in my father and explained what this priest was telling the youth, inviting him to come and listen.

My father didn't brush my concerns aside, but treated them with respect and came with me to the next meeting. Despite his presence, the young priest brought another divisive message and as the night ended and we were all leaving, I said to my father, *"Did you hear what he said?"*

My father nodded his assent, *"Yes, I heard."*

That affirmation was all the encouragement I needed. I walked over to the priest and boldly told him that I was not happy with what he was teaching and the division he was bringing to the group. He didn't argue with me, and I was surprised that he listened to me. I didn't know my father was standing behind me as I spoke. I only realised he was there when I started to fumble my words and I heard his voice behind me quietly say, *"Monnie".* I immediately stopped talking and stepped to the side. I knew my father would take over. As he stepped into the position I had vacated, he continued my train of thought, though with the clarity, authority and wisdom of a man. I was so proud to be his daughter.

I loved what my father did that day. I loved that he encouraged me to try to bring justice where injustice was being done. I loved that he stood behind me and only stepped in when I faltered. My father was such a Godly man. What he did that day is exactly what God does for us. He listens to His children, encourages us, stands behind us as we step out to do His will, and when we begin to stumble or falter, He steps in and completes what we started.

*Your ears will hear this command behind you:
"This is The Way, walk in it." Isaiah 30:21*

A few weeks later, that young priest was gone. Not because of what we said to him, but because God went beyond what we could do and exposed his hidden sin. He voluntarily left the priesthood in order to hastily marry his pregnant, seventeen-year-old girlfriend.

Though I didn't know anything about his private life, I felt justified that I had taken the right decision, with my father's endorsement, to stand up for what was right. I also began to learn how God works with us, and when I can expect to see him move.

A nasty downside!

The downside to this wolfish encounter was a slow sinking. Everything was fine while I was boldly standing up for what was right—it felt like I was walking on water! But afterwards I began to sink.

I began to rationalise and look around at the natural elements involved in this story, the priesthood, the Catholic church, religion, hypocrisy, all the age-old questions and arguments, and I lost faith. Until then, I didn't know my faith was in the Catholic church; I thought my faith was in Christ, but I found out it wasn't. All I had to do was ask my Saviour for help, but I wasn't as smart as the Apostle Peter, so when I started to sink, I just sank. I didn't cry out, *"Lord, save me!" Matthew 14:13*

When I decided I could no longer respect what I'd seen in the Catholic priesthood, I walked away from the Catholic church. That's when I realised I was no better than the young priest I had stood so firmly against.

He had been teaching that only Catholics belonged to God and everyone else was damned to Hell. Now, ironically, as I walked away from the Catholic church, I realised I held exactly the same belief, for I believed with all my heart that as I walked away from Catholicism, I was walking away from God and so was condemning myself to Hell.

I was living the anathema!

For the next seven years, I struggled with the belief that I was cut off from God, hated by him and condemned to Hellfire. I had voluntarily excommunicated myself from the Catholic church and had no intention of returning. This meant I was cursed, and it didn't help that my mother enjoyed throwing coals on the fire of this evil belief.

My theology was as twisted as twisted can be, and I didn't see then how arrogant I was to think I had the power to condemn myself, or anyone else, to Hell. That power belongs only to God, but I didn't see my foolishness; I didn't want to see. I was in darkness and drowning in a sea of self-condemnation, until my Saviour reached down into the dark waters and pulled me to safety. I didn't ask him to help me. He just did!

Foolish self-condemnation!

One night, about seven years after my wolfish encounter, I became acutely aware that there was nothing I could do to make God accept me. I knew I was going to Hell, and there was nothing I could do to prevent it happening. That night, crushing despair engulfed me, and I threw myself down on my bed and wept hard and long. I must have done myself some damage because the following morning, I woke in agony. I couldn't move without a great deal of effort, and my tears burnt my eyes. I didn't know what was wrong, so my flatmate called a doctor.

When the doctor came, his diagnosis was short and to the point. "*It seems you have a hernia about to rupture and a temperature of 104 degrees. Stay in bed until that temperature drops and don't lift anything heavy. If that hernia ruptures, you'll need surgery.*"

Taking the pills the doctor gave me, I went back to sleep. I don't remember much about the next two days, but on the third day, I awoke feeling almost normal and decided I felt well enough to go back to work. Big mistake!

The job I had involved lifting, and though I tried to be careful, I wasn't careful enough. Toward the end of my shift, a ripping pain shot across my waist, but not wanting to believe it was serious, I waited for the pain to subside, finished my shift and went home. That's when my worst fears were realised.

The fever, nausea, and swelling in my stomach were evidence that the hernia could have ruptured. Now I was really in trouble. A wave of disorientation came over me, and I struggled to concentrate on what I should do. My flatmates weren't home, and I was now in too much pain to drive myself to the hospital. I phoned the emergency number, but for some reason it was engaged. Panic set in! I braced myself against the wall and tried to force myself to be logical, but I just couldn't think. I was paralysed with fear and didn't know what to do.

Amazing redemption!

At that moment, there was a knock at my door. My friend Phil was a believer and had just travelled 300 miles to visit me. What a Godsend! What timing! I didn't waste a moment telling him of my predicament, and as I talked, he led me gently to the lounge room and guided me into an armchair. When I was settled, he asked one very earnest question. *"Do you believe God will heal you?"*

His question made me feel dirty, and I shrank down into the armchair, turning my face away from him, *"God wouldn't want to heal me, Phil, I'm just a dirty old sinner."*

He tried asking the same question a different way. *"Do you believe God is able to heal you?"*

My response was immediate, almost angry, *"God can do anything he wants to Phil, he's God!"*

Phil settled himself in the armchair opposite mine and said, *"Well then, let's pray."* He began to pray, and then abruptly stopped. *"I've never done this before, but I've got a book in the car, do you mind if I go and get it?"*

I nodded my head to acknowledge that I didn't mind, and I don't remember thinking anything while he was away. After he returned, Phil once again settled himself in the chair opposite mine, opened his book and began to read.

Suddenly, in one movement, he snapped-closed the book, sprang out of his chair and lunged at me with one hand stretched out in my direction.

I didn't know what to expect, so I gasped and again shrank down in the chair, this time in an attitude of self-protection.

As soon as Phil's open palm found my forehead, he quietly commanded, *"In Christ's name be healed!"* Then, removing his hand from my head, he returned to his chair.

From the time Phil's hand touched my forehead, an amazing sensation began to flow through my body. At first, I thought it was just one of those tingly feelings that come with touch, and knowing those feelings are easily shaken off, I shook my head to see if it would go away. It didn't! I began to realise something unusual was happening.

I was being healed!

The healing seemed to take about twenty minutes, and the experience was like nothing I have ever known before or since. A band, like a wide sash of about 18" deep, wrapped itself around me and slowly descended through my body from head to foot. The band was like a warm mass of soft pins and needles. Where it had been was light as a feather, but where it had not yet reached was still heavy and aching. It worked its way down my body, lingered in the tip of my big toe and was gone. I was totally healed. The headache and temperature were gone, and the swelling and pain in my stomach were gone. I felt light, fit, healthy and totally stunned.

Undeserved acceptance!

Though the healing was an extraordinary miracle, it was nothing at all compared to the powerful reality of God's love and acceptance that seemed to flood the room and my entire being like a thick coating of honey. Now I knew God loved me, that he had not rejected me and that he had forgiven my sins.

Tears of gratitude streamed down my face, and overwhelming joy filled my heart. I was no longer on my way to Hell, and I couldn't thank God enough for releasing me from the Catholic Church's anathema and bringing me into the safety of his loving arms. Instinctively, I knew I had no right to be healed, for I had no faith for healing, no expectation of healing, and didn't even ask for healing, yet in his great mercy, God sovereignly healed me anyway.

The greatest miracle that occurred that night was the revelation of God's total and undeserved acceptance and love for me, a sinner.

God wasn't finished!

Phil and I talked for hours. Then something else happened, something I'd never experienced. The Bible came alive to me! I'd had a Catholic Bible since childhood, but now I suddenly had a strong urge to actually read it! I picked up my Bible and opened it, and a few lines seemed to jump off the page. As it turned out, the words in those lines confirmed the same call of God I'd experienced when I was seven, though upgraded to suit my adult understanding.

> *O God, the wicked are risen up against me, and the assembly of the mighty have sought my soul. They have not set thee before their eyes. Psalm 86:14 Douay-Rheims Bible*

I knew my Redeemer was warning me about the road ahead. I knew I was going to be surrounded by wicked people who would try to destroy me, and that these people would all have one thing in common: *no fear of God before their eyes. Romans 3:12-18.*

Was I prepared to face ogres and wolves again? Did I want to work with the Spirit of God to free *the priesthood of all believers* from the ogre of religion? All I had to do was say 'yes'! I was amazed God would speak to me so directly, but after doing what he had just done for me, I didn't question his assignment. I was not afraid. I was ready.

Anyone
who does not
take up his cross
and follow Me
is not worthy of Me.

- Matthew 10:38 -

Facing the ogres!

CHAPTER 8

Ogres, wolves,
false prophets,
and the
will of God!

STANDING FOR GOD

I had just seen my loving God sovereignly restore seven years of my life that *the locust had eaten Joel 2:25-26,* and I now spent my time joyfully learning about the beauty, power, glory, and accessibility of my faithful, resurrected Saviour. I couldn't learn enough, or fast enough. I witnessed miracles, signs, and wonders and saw firsthand what a true fellowship of genuine believers looked and felt like.

My days were happy, yet the strong word God had brought alive to me on the day of my healing was burnt into my consciousness. Being *surrounded by wicked people who would attack my soul* was not something I was eagerly looking forward to, yet even in my spiritual innocence, I knew it would become real in my life. I knew that no matter how long it would take to happen, it would happen! God had planted that truth in my heart, and I believed it.

> *For the vision awaits an appointed time; it testifies of the end and does not lie. Though it lingers, wait for it, since it will surely come and will not delay.* Habakkuk 2:3

When I look back now, some fifty years later, over the tapestry of my life, I can see that from the very beginning, various parts of the already written word of God were slowly fitting themselves together like pieces of a puzzle to create a solid picture of the call of God on my life. The words He gave me would each become real as my experiences unfolded.

My Saviour was sending me out again, as he did when I was young, as a sheep among wolves, only this time some of the wolves would be people I knew and loved. In the past, I had only faced one ogre and one wolf. Now, I was going to be surrounded!

This time, also, I would be on my own and not have my earthly father backing me up, for within a year, my beloved father would be dead. It wasn't until God removed my father that the ogres, wolves and false prophets began to gather.

> *I am sending you out like sheep among wolves. Therefore, be as wise as serpents and as innocent as doves.*
>
> *Be on your guard; you will be handed over to the local councils and be flogged in the synagogues.*
>
> *On my account, you will be brought before governors and kings as witnesses to them and to the Gentiles.*
>
> *When they arrest you, do not worry about what to say. At that time, you will be given what to say, for it will not be you speaking, but the Spirit of God speaking through you.*
>
> *Brother will betray brother to death, and a father his child; children will rebel against their parents and have them put to death.*
>
> *You will be hated by everyone because of me, but the one who stands firm to the end will be saved.*
>
> *When they persecute you in one town, flee to the next. You will not reach all the towns of Israel before the Son of Man returns.*

It is enough for a disciple to be like his teacher. If the head of the house is called Beelzebul, how much more the members of his household!

So do not be afraid of them. For nothing is concealed that will not be uncovered, or hidden that will not be made known.

What I tell you in the dark, speak in the light; what I whisper, proclaim from the housetops.

Do not be afraid of those who kill the body but cannot kill the soul. Instead, fear the One who can destroy both soul and body in Hell. Matthew 10:16-28

Over the last five decades, every one of the above verses has become real, or flesh, in my life. I have learned the hard way that these verses are an accurate description of what wolves, false prophets and pretenders living comfortably with the ogre of religion will do to the royal priesthood of believers who strive to follow The Way of Christ.

I discovered quickly that the religious counterfeit to The Way of Christ, the apostasy set up by Constantine, was no longer confined to the Catholic church, but had spread like a cancer to every other denomination which had supposedly broken away from Catholicism. These new denominations were merely a change of name, for the structure they supported; buildings, pulpits, ministry overlords, ritualistic worship services, and liturgical controls were identical to Constantine's. Though the 'religion' is called Christianity, followers of The Way of Christ are still not welcome in their gatherings.

Below is a brief overview of what I have experienced at the hands of those who call themselves 'Christians'. This is what *wickedness* looks like and what an *attack on the soul* feels like. I personally call myself a believer and follower of Christ's Way, and I would go through all this again if I had to. It is my joy to serve my Lord.

God knows I am speaking the truth!

In my lifetime, I have been beaten many times. I have had hard objects thrown at me. I have had my clothes ripped off so violently that the cloth burns marked my skin for seven years.

For three months, I was dragged out of bed by my hair before dawn each day and ordered to worship the rising sun. When I refused, and I always did, I was beaten.

Once, I was dragged along the ground by my arm for over 25 meters. My arm was severely damaged and took two years to heal.

I was accused of 'controlling God' and ordered not to pray. If I was found praying, I was beaten.

I was ordered not to sing praises, and my guitar was smashed. If I was found singing, I was beaten.

If I was found sitting down when I could be working, I was beaten.

If I was found crying, I would be beaten. For many years, the only place I could cry safely was in the shower; even then, my face was 'inspected' for tears.

I have had the life of my unborn child threatened while seven months pregnant for not being able to 'forgive' my previous beating quickly enough.

I have been betrayed by family, by friends, by ministers who claim to be Christ's, but are not.

I have been stolen from, lied about, insulted, slandered, abused and labelled a child of Satan.

I have been called before a council of elders for daring to question a particular church doctrine.

I have been called to act as a witness for Christ in front of people in high office and the National leader.

I have been called evil in front of my children for the 'sin' of disagreeing with a pastor's wife.

When I spoke the truth, I was called a liar. When I offered kindness and the love of God, I was accused of trying to control. When I forgave with all my heart, I was mocked as a fool.

The words of Paul, in *2 Corinthians 6:11,* became real in my life and so now, like Paul, I can honestly stand before my God and say that I understand what it's like to be punished yet not killed; sorrowful yet always rejoicing; poor yet able to make others rich, owning nothing and yet possessing everything. Like Paul, I have learned to rejoice in my sufferings, hardships, calamities and weaknesses because they were the narrow way to God's power.

Forgiveness became a constant and natural state of mind. And out of forgiveness came the comfort of deep peace and a profound love for Christ.

Though I was forbidden to pray and sing praise, I learned to pray and praise without ceasing. No matter what I was doing, I had a song in my heart, and all my thoughts went to God as prayers.

This was not my doing. I can't claim any righteousness in this. This was a gift from God. It was the manifestation of his promise that during times of persecution, his Spirit of Glory would rest on those being persecuted. When I was weak, he was strong for me, as promised.

> *If you are insulted because of the Name of Christ, you are blessed, for the Spirit of Glory and of God rests on you. 1 Peter 4:14-16*

Then the miracles began!

During this time, I saw God work through my prayers in ways which could only be explained as miraculous. I knew we were all commissioned, so I found myself healing the sick, raising the dead and casting out demons, but that was only the beginning. I discovered that the authority given to *the priesthood of all believers* is immense.

The first healing...

The first child I saw God heal through prayer was a five-year-old who had suffered a bad reaction to epilepsy drugs. His little body was so swollen with fluid, he could only move his eyes and the tips of his fingers. Then his kidneys failed him completely, and he went into a coma.

The hospital doctors told his mother they couldn't do anything for him, and if he survived, he would most likely remain in a vegetative state.

The first time I asked his mother if I could pray for him, she said "no". On hearing this news, I asked her again. This time she said "yes". So I went to the hospital chapel. I found out later that at the time I was praying, this little boy came out of his coma, sat up in bed and told the nurse he was hungry.

This young boy's healing was so unusual and thorough that the miraculous nature of his recovery was reported in a major Sydney paper as a reason for people to donate money to support the hospital's ongoing work.

The second healing...

The second child was a seven-year-old in a Meningitis-induced coma. When I told her mother about the first child, she asked me to pray for her child, and we prayed together for her daughter.

Within half an hour, the little girl came out of her coma. After tests, it was revealed she was completely healed, with no side effects from the Meningitis. Her mother gave God the glory.

The third healing...

The third child was my nine-year-old son. Stephen had jumped off the roof of the garden shed onto the trampoline and had been catapulted to a nearby gum tree, where he became impaled.

His cousins climbed up and removed him from the tree. When they brought him inside, it took a while for my sister Julia and I to work out where he was hurt, for there was no blood, and Stephen was in shock. We finally discovered a deep gash under his arm and took him straight to the hospital.

While we were waiting for the doctor, the nurse cleaned his wound and told us it was very deep and would need stitches. Stephen was so distressed by the cleaning he begged, *"I don't want stitches, Mum, don't let them give me stitches"*. I put my hand on his head and prayed for God's peace. As soon as my hand touched his head, he fell into a deep sleep. When the doctor arrived forty-five minutes later, he couldn't open the wound. It was sealed tight. God had heard my son's cry. He was completely healed. There would be no stitches for Stephen.

Raised from the dead...

I had taken my youngest son, Martin, to the clinic as his nose had started bleeding and wouldn't stop. This had never happened to him before and has never happened since. My sister Kathleen, who was visiting us, accompanied me to the clinic.

While we were sitting in the waiting area, a distressed young mother came running through the door with an uncommonly pale baby in her arms, begging, *"My baby can't breathe...please save my baby."* The nursing staff tended to her immediately. The baby was only a few months old.

My sister and I started praying for the baby, and had been praying for about ten minutes when a nurse announced the clinic would be closing and directed everyone to another clinic. Meanwhile, an ambulance arrived.

It was obvious from the tone of the nurse's voice that they had not been able to revive the infant. I looked down at my son. His nosebleed had stopped. He was fine. Of course, I knew by now we were not there for a nosebleed; we were there because a baby needed prayer.

At that moment, the mother and baby, and a doctor and nurse, bustled through the clinic and out to the waiting ambulance.

The baby's father had arrived with the baby's pram and was being denied access to the ambulance. He was upset, *"But I don't have a car, I need to be with my wife and child."* Although the medical staff were sympathetic, they would not allow him to enter the ambulance.

I glanced at my sister and though no words were spoken, we were in agreement. Kathleen went over and asked the young man if he would like a ride to the hospital. He nearly wept with gratitude, but there was no time for talk; we had to hurry.

We folded the pram into the boot, and the baby's father sat in the back of the sedan with Martin, who was now showing no sign of a nosebleed. We took off for the hospital, a fifteen-minute drive.

As we drove along, the young father told us what had happened. The doctors had not been able to revive his baby. They thought there was something lodged in her throat, but they couldn't find anything to dislodge. They were now taking the baby to the hospital to put a camera tube down her neck to see where the blockage was situated. He began to cry, *"It's too late! It's been too long!"*

I told him we believed in the power of prayer, that Christ had the power to raise his daughter from death, that faith as tiny as a mustard seed was all that was needed, and that we could pray that God would do a miracle while we were driving.

He stopped crying and told us he used to be a believer but had lost his faith. I asked him if he would mind if we prayed for his daughter, and he begged us, *"Oh yes, please pray"*. My sister began to sing praise, and I began to pray.

After about ten minutes of singing and praying, the young man joined in. With tears, he asked God's forgiveness for turning away from him and beseeched him for the life of his baby girl.

When he finished praying, a heavy blanket of peace filled the car. It was the same as the honey blanket I had felt on the day I was healed. I didn't have to tell the young father about the peace in the car; it was so heavy, the young man told us he could feel it. Then, I explained that the peace he could feel was proof that God had answered his prayer.

The timing was amazing, for the peace of God settled heavily on us just as we entered the hospital grounds. I drove up to the emergency entrance, and without a parting word, the young father opened the door, jumped out of the car and ran into the hospital.

As I still had his baby's pram, I parked the car so we could take the pram into the hospital. My sister was just setting the pram onto the ground when the young man came rushing back to us, gushing, crying, praising God and completely beside himself.

"She's ok! She's alive! She's breathing!" He could hardly speak between sobs. *"This is the second time we've nearly lost her…last time I hated God, but now…this is a miracle! She hasn't been breathing for over forty minutes…they couldn't revive her…but she suddenly coughed and started breathing a few minutes ago, and the doctors don't know why…they couldn't find any blockage…they don't know why she started breathing again!"*

The young man stood with us and praised God in the car park, and then he took us inside to meet his wife and three-month-old baby girl. He told the doctors, nurses, his parents, and friends who had gathered, as well as anyone who would listen, that God had performed a miracle! His baby was alive!

God heard a young father's prayers that night and saved two lives: the baby's and her father's. I was humbled to be part of this glorious miracle of salvation. A miracle of Christ, for the glory of God.

The tip of the iceberg...

These four testimonies are the tip of the iceberg. I can't count all the miracles, signs, wonders and answered prayers I've experienced in my life so far.

Many times, I've been met by angels; they just seem to turn up when I need a helping hand.

Many times, I've seen God turn people around in mid-stride, or change their minds mid-sentence.

Many times, I've had miraculous provision, and been the giver of miraculous provision.

I've been led to be in the right place at the right time so many times I can't count them all.

More than once, I've seen prayer remove the unrighteous from a high office or political position.

More than once, I've quoted Scriptures I didn't know existed until I looked them up later.

More than once, I've had dreams that have come to pass the next day.

More than once, I've seen God totally transform people by the power of His Spirit.

Once, I witnessed God open the spiritual eyes of two hundred children in a few weeks.

Once, I was diagnosed with cancer and then healed so that God could witness to a non-believer.

Once, I was used by God to slay a giant as I stood against massive political corruption.

Several times, I have witnessed the Spirit of God cast out demons. And three times I have seen God's powerful judgment fall onto pretenders in the church who were blatantly dishonouring him.

When I first saw God dealing with pretenders, I was shocked. I'm not shocked anymore. God is Holy, and He doesn't like those who trample Christ's Holy Covenant under their feet.

> *How much more severely do you think one deserves to be punished who has trampled on the Son of God, profaned the blood of the Covenant that sanctified him, and insulted the Spirit of grace? For we know Him who said, "Vengeance is Mine; I will repay," and again, "The Lord will judge His people." It is a fearful thing to fall into the hands of the living God. Hebrews 10:29-31*

What I saw God do...

One day, a minister, standing in the pulpit, laughed as he told the congregation how he prepared for Sunday service. He said that each Saturday night, he would clear his lounge room of furniture and get himself rolling drunk. Some of the people in the pews laughed with him; some didn't. I was horrified! But that's not what shocked me. It was the way God dealt with him that shocked me.

When I arrived home, I immediately began to pray earnestly that God would either change this man's heart or move him away from the people he was deceiving. God's answer was swift.

A few days later, that minister had a heart attack. He didn't die, but neither did he return to ministry. I was deeply shocked. I didn't know that would happen when I prayed with concern for God to protect his people from this man.

> *When you are assembled in the name of our Lord Jesus and I am with you in spirit, along with the power of the Lord Jesus, hand this man over to Satan for the destruction of the flesh, so that his spirit may be saved on the Day of the Lord. 1 Corinthians 5:4-5*

Though I didn't pray for anything bad to happen to this wolf, I did place him into God's hands, and God handed him over to Satan for the destruction of his body, just as Scripture says. I was learning...

Seven years later...

The second time, seven years later, was completely different. I had been attending a large, wealthy church for some time. Then, one night at home, my children's bedroom caught fire. It was a faulty electric blanket. By God's grace, my children were not in their room that night, but were safe in my room, having a 'sleepover' with me.

The beds and bedding were destroyed, the walls were covered in yellow gunk, as were their books and toys, most of which would now have to be thrown away. I didn't have the money to replace their beds and bedding, but God always provided my needs, and I was so confident that He would provide again that I didn't even ask for provision.

That's why I was surprised when God clearly told me to go to the minister of the church I attended and ask for financial assistance. I said, *"No, Lord! I have never asked for anything from a church; I have only given."* He told me to go and ask for assistance a second time, and again, I argued, *"They won't give anything to me, Lord, I know they won't."*

When the Lord spoke to me a third time, the penny dropped. God already knew they wouldn't help me, and that's why he was sending me.

> *I have made you a tester of metals and my people the ore, that you may observe and test their ways. The bellows blow fiercely to burn away the dross with fire, but the refining goes on in vain; the wicked are not purged out. Jeremiah 6:27-29*

I now understood that God's faithful ones in that congregation had cried out to God about the leadership of that church, and now he wanted to put the leadership to the test. This is the wickedness he had told me I would encounter. I agreed to go.

I knew I was walking into humiliation and shame. I knew my request for financial assistance would be rejected. I also knew that God wanted to give them a chance, so I couldn't let them know they were being tested. I went in gentle humility three times, and three times I was subjected to a string of arrogant, self-righteous, probing, embarrassing and unnecessary personal questions, only to walk away humiliated and empty-handed.

What this wolf-in-sheep's-clothing didn't realise was that I wasn't the one he needed to worry about. It was the one standing behind me that mattered. And my *fearful living God* was already on his case.

As soon as I left the church office for the third time, before I even got to the car park, I looked up into the sky and said, *"Well, Lord, you heard, you saw, now I hand them over to you."*

The following week, God provided all my needs and more. From a vastly different and unexpected source, I was given enough funds to refurbish my children's bedroom and replace many of their books and toys. How good is my God!

A few months later, I learned that the head minister of that church had been arrested and charged with embezzlement of church funds. He was later convicted and jailed.

I didn't know any of this about that pretender. I didn't need to know. God knew. God asked me to be His tester and to actively work with Him so that He could answer the prayers of His hurting people. He needed someone to see the problem and hand it over to Him. When I did, God moved immediately. A pattern was beginning to form. I was learning...

Another seven years later...

The third time, another seven years later, was different again. I learned that God loves variety and rarely does the same thing the same way twice, which is why we need to be led by His Spirit

I had been the worship leader of a small church for over four years. The pastor and his wife were business owners who supported themselves, and the church was rented, not owned, so there were no money issues. But that was about to change.

The pastor and his wife decided to sell their business and rely on God's people to support them. And the change began.

They were suddenly on a lower income and their lifestyle was starting to suffer, so they began to seek more money from their small congregation; constantly teaching about tithing and inviting guest speakers to convince everyone to tithe.

This drive for tithes didn't worry me, that is, until one day when a guest speaker began pointing out people in the congregation as examples of those under God's blessing for tithing and those under God's curse for not tithing. I was appalled!

This disgusting betrayal of Christ's sacrifice, breach of people's privacy, and humiliating, public persecution of believers inside a church, during a service, was the worst thing I had witnessed in any church in my life, and I'd seen some awful things.

After the service, I approached the pastor and shared my concerns, reminding him that Christ had taken our curses upon himself on the cross. He didn't want to know and brushed off my concerns. Nevertheless, a few days later, I received a letter summoning me to an elders' meeting at his home.

The strangest thing about that summons was that this small church didn't have any elders. When I arrived at the meeting, I discovered four elders had been hastily appointed, including the pastor's daughter and her newly converted boyfriend.

When the meeting started, I was given the opportunity to share my concerns, and so took them through the notes I had prepared, showing from Scripture that Christ had redeemed us from the curse of the Law. When I finished speaking, the pastor pushed my paperwork away, closed his Bible and said, *"We don't have to go by the written word; we can follow the spirit."*

I was shocked by his words. As Christ is the Word of God made flesh, I now knew the 'spirit' this minister was following was not the Spirit of Christ, and I left that meeting with a broken heart.

That night, I prayed in humility and love that the fire of God's holiness would fall upon them, causing them to burn with passionate love for Christ and the freedom he bought with His great sacrifice.

From that night on, I was persecuted by them, but prayed with all my heart that they would be forgiven, renewed and blessed. The effect of their persecution of me was so bad that I packed up my children and moved to a different State.

Within a year of that meeting, news came to me that the pastor's treasured home and most of his possessions had been burnt to the ground.

I recalled the prayer I prayed as I left their home that night, that God's holy fire would fall on them, but I didn't expect this. I didn't pray for this. I loved this man and his wife and prayed God's holy blessing on them. Yet, here I was, twelve months later, witnessing God literally pour burning coals onto their heads.

> *Love your enemies; bless those who curse you and pray for those who mistreat you. Luke 6:28*
>
> *If your enemy is hungry, feed him; if he is thirsty, give him drink. For in so doing, you will heap burning coals on his head. Romans 12:20*

Three times in three different ways, God showed me how to work with his mighty Spirit to stand against the dishonour and deceit of wicked pretenders who used their pulpits to deceive the elect. This is what he had called me to do from the age of seven. Seek out the true priesthood and identify the wicked religious ogres that try to block their way. The religious ogres I encountered had made themselves enemies of God. And He, Himself, had dealt with them.

Usually, I paid a personal cost each time God asked me to work with His Spirit on some project. But I knew the uncomfortable price I paid was nothing compared to the weight of insults being constantly and unjustly heaped on my Saviour by the soul-destroying wickedness done in the name of 'Christianity'. It may be his name, but it's not his Way.

> *See to it that no one deceives you, for many will come in my name. Matthew 24:4-5*

The Great Misnomer!

Calling what Constantine founded 'Christianity' was the greatest misnomer of all time. What he established was not 'Christianity' but 'churchianity'. The pseudo-religion he built was designed to discourage people from following Christ and obeying his Commission. It was built to corral people under the banner of a denomination, a building or a religion, and swear allegiance to the one who heads the denomination, controls the pulpit or runs the service.

Constantine's 'churchianity' blueprint, upheld through the various denominations that have since adopted his system of domination over *the priesthood of all believers*, was never designed to teach people to submit to Christ and the leading of the mighty Spirit of God. It was never intended to teach people to follow The Way of Christ or obey his Commission.

The epitome of apostasy!

Constantine deliberately launched a religious counterfeit to The Way of Christ for the purpose of controlling the activities of all religions. This is the exact definition of apostasy. Everyone who joined his new one-world religion was required *to abandon or renounce allegiance to any other religion or belief*. The apostasy he established spread like a cancer across the world. Today, thousands of government-sanctioned 'Christian' denominations, based on Constantine's apostate clergy system, continue to promote 'churchianity' over the Way of Christ.

They will
turn their ears
away from the truth
and turn aside
to myths.

- 2 Timothy 4:4 -

Apostle or Apostate?

CHAPTER 9

Does the demise of
Apostles
coincide with
the rise of Apostates?

CANCEROUS APOSTASY

Cancers are caused by the invasion of carcinogens, which mutilate cells, causing catastrophic damage. The singular purpose of carcinogenic invasion is to spread death throughout the body.

Likewise, Constantinian apostasy can be described as the invasion of ideologies which mutilate truth, causing catastrophic damage. The singular purpose of Constantinian apostasy was to spread death throughout the body of Christ.

Seven known symptoms!

In the same way that there are seven medically identified symptoms of cancer, so too, there are seven spiritually identified symptoms of apostasy.

The first symptom...

The mythical development of an 'apostolic age' is the most destructive and invasive of the introduced heretical ideologies. It promotes the false notion that the signs and wonders which accompanied the preaching of the Gospel were limited to the leadership of the first twelve disciples of Christ and ceased at the death of the Apostle John.

This outright lie promotes the blasphemous concept that Christ had no idea what he was doing when he founded his church. It strips him of wisdom and makes him appear foolish.

This myth is like saying God created Adam and Steve and commanded them to fill the world with people, not knowing that Adam and Steve could never have children. What an insult to God!

Christ did not establish His Great Commission for just one generation. That belief is an insult to Christ! The Great Commission can't be limited to one generation, as it is self-perpetuating by its very nature. The Commission is, *Go and make disciples of all nations, teaching them to obey everything I have commanded you*. Everything includes miracles, signs and wonders.

The first disciples obeyed this Commission with signs and wonders following, and they taught others to obey it with signs and wonders following, who then taught others to obey it with signs and wonders following, and so on. The only way this Commission could not have continued is if the first disciples had disobeyed Christ and refused to make disciples. We know that didn't happen!

My question is, where is the evidence that the preaching of the Gospel with signs and wonders following stopped at the death of the Apostle John? Christ did not rescind this command. It is still in effect. This myth is the brainchild of apostates who have no clue how to be disciples of Christ.

> *Woe to you, experts in the Law, because you have taken away the key to knowledge. You yourselves have not entered, and you have hindered those who were entering. Luke 11:52*

The second symptom...

The myth that twelve of Christ's disciples were 'super apostles' specialising in miracles is appalling. It ignores the other 108 people in the Upper Room who received the same power as these twelve to do miracles. Any person who believes the Super Apostle myth doesn't understand that the Spirit of God did the miracles, not the twelve. Those who preach this lie immediately identify as apostate.

This myth is like saying God only used miracles to jump-start his new religion in the same way doctors use a jolt of electricity to jump-start a heart. This myth heretically presumes that God's goal in sending Christ was the creation of a church, when it was always the salvation of people.

Christ did not die and return to life so that a church could be built to commemorate him. He was not seeking a monument; he was seeking hearts. To believe anything else insults his life-giving sacrifice!

The miraculous signs that still accompany the preaching of Christ's Gospel are the normal work of the Spirit of God. The Spirit of God permeates every aspect of the church built by Christ from the foundation up, and that will never change. This myth can only be the brainchild of apostates who do not preach the Gospel of Christ, but another Gospel.

Woe to you because you are like unmarked graves which men walk over without knowing it. Luke 11.44

The third symptom...

The mythical 'good people go to Heaven' teaching was designed to replace the New Covenant promise of eternal life. Human works were exalted by those who had no signs and wonders accompanying their preaching. This false teaching was heavily promoted by the clergy class, who desired high honour and praise despite their lack of spiritual power.

This myth intimates that all good people, and even good animals, 'go to Heaven' without the slightest hint that eternal life is a reward for allowing the Spirit of God to do the ministry work of Christ in this world.

Preachers who promote this broadly believed religious lie simultaneously reject the work of the Spirit of God and Christ's testimony that the work of the Spirit is the rock on which his church will be built. Their false teachings and lack of Spirit-powered works identify them as apostate.

Eternal life, Heaven and all their associated blessings can only be accessed by those who submit to the leading of God's mighty Spirit.

This Godless myth is the brainchild of powerless apostates who want to appear righteous, but don't know how to allow the Spirit of God to do the work of Christ through them.

> *Woe to you because you love the most important seats in the synagogues and greetings in the marketplaces. Luke 11:43*

The fourth symptom...

The blasphemous myth that 'spiritual gifts' are of the devil and should not be sought by thinking Christians is one of the greatest lies ever told. The supernatural power of the Spirit given to the church at Pentecost could only be made available to mere humans after the resurrection of Christ. They are a treasure of heaven, more precious than anything on this earth. Those who deny the gifts of the Spirit immediately identify as apostate.

The horrible teaching that the gifts of God's Spirit, like tongues, prophesy, miracles and wonders are of the devil completely denies God's power, God's will, God's Commandments, Christ's Way and everything written by the Apostles in the Gospels, Epistles and the Book of Revelation.

Preachers who promote these lies do not want anyone to work with the Spirit to build Christ's church because they want to promote their own religion. However, if the gates of Hell cannot prevail against God's Spirit, then mere lies don't stand a chance.

This myth is the brainchild of apostates who love to keep busy with good works, but show no love for God and the works He wants His Spirit to do.

> *Woe to you because you give God a tenth of your mint, rue and all other kinds of garden herbs, but you neglect justice and the love of God. You should have practised the latter without leaving the former undone. Luke 11.4*

The fifth symptom...

The myth that having a 'good reputation' would be more desirable than spiritual manifestations became a playground for wolves and pretenders. By insisting that God's work be performed without the Spirit's help, apostates created burdens far too heavy for the faithful to bear. Manipulation through created burdens is the gameplay of apostates.

Christ came to take our burdens from us. *Come to me, all you who are weary and burdened, and I will give you rest. Take my yoke upon you and learn from me; for I am gentle and humble in heart, and you will find rest for your souls. Matthew 11:28-29.*

Religious burdens are laid on people in subtle, underhanded ways through implied condemnation, innuendo, peer pressure, pointed remarks, and unspoken expectations. They are designed to weigh us down, make us subservient, keep us dependent on the clergy class, and rob us of our authority.

However, the Spirit of God is always available to empower God's word through every believer, so that we can shake off religious burdens and the snare of imputed reputation. This myth is the brainchild of apostates who seek to keep people dependent on them rather than on God.

> *And you, experts in the Law, woe to you because you load people down with burdens they can hardly carry, and you yourselves will not lift one finger to help them. Luke 11.46*

The sixth symptom...

The myth that Christ's 'command to go' ended with the death of the Apostle John was a perfect way to stop people from 'going'. Much better to keep them captive in pews. Under Constantine, 'going' was replaced with enforced conversions, allowing his religion to grow quickly. Later, 'going' was done by official 'missionaries' in the name of their denomination. In these ways, 'going' was effectively repurposed to create converts to a religion rather than converts to The Way of Christ. This sneaky sleight of hand is the epitome of apostasy.

Christ told his disciples not to 'go' in their own strength, but to wait until they were sealed with God's Spirit and empowered to go, *Acts 1:4-5*. Once they were filled, they could go in the authority of Christ's name to do the work of the Spirit. This was God's recipe for success. It was His idea!

The myth that God suddenly and without reason changed his mind and cancelled the Great Commission, even though there is absolutely no confirming evidence of this anywhere in Scripture, is pure apostasy. This myth can only be the brainchild of apostates who seek converts to their denominational name instead of Christ's name.

> *Woe to you, teachers of the Law, you hypocrites! You travel over land and sea to win a single convert, and when you have succeeded, you make them twice as much a child of Hell as you are. Matthew 23:15*

The seventh symptom...

The myth that the early disciples needed to establish a system of priests, bishops, deacons, and missionaries as a means of organising the growing number of believers is the rationale used by apostates to explain away their lack of faith in Christ and unwillingness to trust the Spirit of God.

The reality is, Constantine cemented over the foundation built by the apostles, established an entirely new belief system on the foundation of the Roman Empire, and told everyone his new religion was built on the foundation of the apostles.

It didn't seem to matter that the very 'saints' extolled by his new religion were slaughtered by the same brutal regime now perversely exalting them as saints. It didn't seem to matter that the foundation cemented over was covered in the blood of those who died cruel deaths at the hands of the Roman Empire. It didn't seem to matter to Constantine that in cementing over the foundation laid by Christ, he was crucifying Christ all over again.

This myth is the brainchild of apostates who need to keep apostolic teaching obsolete lest their own faithless dismissal of Christ betray them.

> *Woe to you because you build tombs for the prophets, and it was your forefathers who killed them. So you testify that you approve of what your forefathers did; they killed the prophets, and you build the tombs. Luke 11:47-51*

Killing the Body!

Constantine's apostasy spread like a cancer around the known world. Fuelled by a heavy-handed system of rewards and punishments, his new State-controlled religion, generally known as 'Christianity', flourished, not as a religion but as a political tool.

As the Roman influence spread, so did Christianity. For hundreds of years, conquered kings could not rule without papal advice. Despite being named Christianity, this new Roman religion showed no connection to the name it had stolen, and so the name of Christ gradually became associated with typically recognised Roman political atrocities.

Historically, we know of crusaders, who massacred anyone who opposed them; witch hunters, who tortured, tore apart and burned at the stake; missionaries who brutalised natives into submission; slave drivers, who bought, sold and abused slaves, mobs of Catholics, who persecuted Jews that refused to convert; clergy who sexually abused children; inquisitors who tortured suspected heretics after forced conversions and murdered scientists who deviated from church dogma. Even today, there are clergy within all denominations who still slaughter by slander anyone who won't conform to their particular creeds, still pressure people into giving money, and still force women to remain in violent or dangerous relationships to prove their faith.

This is not The Way of Christ!

The Roman Empire, under Constantine, altered apostolic doctrine to control and corral the followers of Christ within a State-run religion. Those who joined the new Imperial religion did so under threat of persecution or death. They didn't have a choice. Anyone who dared question the new apostate teaching was tortured or executed. Many who called themselves 'Christian' had no interest in salvation from sin, only salvation from torture and death, even if it meant killing people simply because they were enemies of Rome.

Constantine's pseduo-Christianity also exploited those who truly believed in God and Christ by using them to gain wealth and spread Rome's power and influence. Under threat of reprisal, many were forced to kill, steal and destroy for the sake of the Roman Empire. No longer did Roman soldiers need to fight all the wars or do all the torturing. They were now greatly assisted by conscripts from Christianity.

An effective spy network!

The vast and efficient control of so many individuals across continents didn't happen by accident. In typical Roman Imperial style, it was planned and executed with military precision. Every gathering of 'Christians' had a spy in the camp, someone with the authority of a military officer, or tribune, who would report back to the Emperor and keep the individual congregational members in check. The symbol of Rome's overt and accepted Imperial authority was the dias, which later became known as the pulpit.

There is
nothing hidden
from him
to whom we
must give account.

- Hebrew 4:13 -

Tribunes Of Rome!

CHAPTER 10

Tribunal
was the name
given to
a dias, a rostrum,
a raised gallery area
or a pulpit!

DECEPTIVE TRIBUNES

A brief study of the Roman Empire and its predecessor, the Roman Republic, reveals some shocking truths about the structure of Constantine's State-run religion. We are what we know, and Constantine was a soldier of Rome.

A concise history!

Prior to the Republic, Rome was a monarchy, but in 509BC, the wealthy families seized control. Fifty oligarchs created a power cooperative, which they called a *Senate*. From there, they controlled the appointment of *magistrates, military officers* and *priests*, using their absolute power to increase their landholdings and oppress the rest of society.

Roman citizens, called *'plebeians'*, had only one option open to them to fight the brutal oppression of the wealthy Senators, *'secessio plebis'*, the cessation of labour and services to the wealthy. This is what we call 'strike action', and it worked! Through their strikes, the people gained protection under both civil and religious laws, as well as the right to vote. That vote was called a *'plebiscite'*.

Once they could vote, the people elected plebeian representatives to the Senate, who had the power to veto unwelcome decisions. These representatives were called *'tribunes'*.

Tribunes were the voice of the people!

The election of tribunes led to decades of political infighting inside the Senate until the tribunes finally succumbed to the will of the wealthy oligarchs.

Once united, the tribunes and oligarchs became the 'elites' of Rome, and their combined new goal was to increase landholdings and personal wealth through the conquest of surrounding nations.

Wars became normal. As each nation fell, the elites selected and installed 'puppet-leaders' from within each fallen nation who would, for financial reward, willingly serve the Roman Republic rather than their own people.

As the wealth and power of both tribunes and oligarchs grew, so did their corruption and self-interest, and it wasn't long before laws were made for the interests of the few ruling elites rather than for the good of the people of the Republic.

Moral decay, chaos, instability, famine, slavery and the rise of widespread social unrest became the new normal in the Roman Republic until the people said 'enough' and active plans to overthrow the corrupt government system led to civil war.

After a century of social unrest, insurrections and civil war, the Roman Republic collapsed in 27BC and was replaced by the Roman Empire. It was basically a return to the monarchy system, though with an elected Emperor instead of a King.

The role of tribune changed!

The Emperor now had autonomous control over the appointment of *magistrates, military officers* and *priests*, and absolute power over the rest of society.

The Senate's ability to influence government was diminished, and, although it continued to exist, the role of a Senator became nothing more than a symbol of social standing, open only to the very wealthy and high-born social classes.

Tribunes no longer had a voice!

When Constantine decided to establish his new State-run religion, he revived the role of tribune, but with strict controls. Some military officers in remote outposts had been granted the authority to act on behalf of the Emperor as magistrates, and since the Empire's inception, officers with this authority had been referred to as tribunes. Now, Constantine extended that right to non-military tribunes who would oversee his various new religious 'outposts'.

The people would not elect these tribunes; instead, like military officer tribunes, they would be appointed by the State and equipped with the legal authority (credentials) to act on behalf of the State.

Since Constantine modelled his new religion on the structure of the Roman Empire, his first four religious tribunes were sent to oversee the four major geographical areas of his Imperial rule. Once endowed with the high title of *Pontifex* (bishop), these four tribunes carried the Imperial authority of the Roman Empire and Constantine himself.

When Constantine later built his four historic basilicas in those areas, the raised gallery under the dome was specifically designed as a symbol of authority, elevating those on the raised platform to a position higher than everyone else. When a tribune entered the tribunal or pulpit, his voice carried the authority of the Emperor. He was not there to speak for the people or for God; he was there for the State.

Apostate authority!

From the very beginning, pulpits were designed as an authority structure, to keep the masses subservient to the religion and its overlords, ensure conformity to the new apostate doctrines, enforce religious 'donations', and spy on adherents, bringing swift reprisals for those who dissented.

Pulpits were never designed to be *'a spout where the glory comes out'*. There has never been anything holy or glorious about them or the people who stand in them. They were never designed to encourage people to serve Christ or follow his Way.

One of the great ongoing lies of the Constantinian legacy is that those who stand in pulpits are superior to everyone else. Their words are regarded as more wise or holy than those of ordinary people. They are seen to be somehow closer to God, more able to speak about the things of God, and more willing to do his will than the rest of us can ever hope to be.

That is hardcore religious indoctrination!

The widespread belief that credentialed clergy who stand in pulpits somehow have more authority or more holiness or more spiritual experience than the rest of us is mere performance training. It is a clear and present relic of Constantinian apostasy.

Pulpits represent apostasy!

Have you ever wondered why people who desire to preach from a pulpit need to first obtain a credential from a Bible College or seminary affiliated with their chosen religious denomination? Have you ever wondered why Christ chose twelve men as his disciples who were not trained in religious dogma? Jesus explained his decision to his disciples when he said this about the religious class.

> *Though seeing, they do not see; though hearing, they do not hear or understand.*
>
> *In them, the prophecy of Isaiah is fulfilled: 'You will be ever hearing but never understanding; you will be ever seeing but never perceiving.*
>
> *For this people's heart has grown callous; they hardly hear with their ears, and they have closed their eyes.*
>
> *Otherwise, they might see with their eyes, hear with their ears, understand with their hearts, and turn, and I would heal them'.*
> *Matthew 13:14-15*

The pulpit is Constantine's most devious apostate legacy. It was, and still is, the 'control centre' of his entire operation. Without the pulpit, the fraudulent pseudo-religion he set up would crumble and fall.

Evidence of unbelief!

Today, every person who stands in a pulpit preaches in the authority of their religion rather than in the authority of Christ. They can't serve two masters! To those who follow Christ's Way, the pulpit is an abomination that cries loudly, proclaiming that the person standing in it has chosen to submit to Constantine's widespread apostasy rather than follow the narrow path encouraged by Christ.

> *For the time is coming when men will not tolerate sound doctrine, but with itching ears they will gather around themselves teachers to suit their own desires. 2 Timothy 4:3*
>
> *God will send on them a powerful delusion so that they believe the lie, in order that judgment may come upon all who have disbelieved the truth and instead have delighted in wickedness. 2 Thessalonians 2:11-12*

Truth overcomes the lie!

The Roman Empire, even at the height of its power, could not prevent genuine followers of Christ from growing and spreading the Great Commission. It was because they couldn't overcome the Gospel that they had to try to drown it in confusion, illusion, controversy and lies. Even so, centuries later, Christ's Great Commission still stands, and those who love him still obey his teaching, still carry his Spirit, still do miracles, signs and wonders, and still use the seven powerful keys of his kingdom to overcome all Satan's deceptions, including apostasy.

Choose
for yourselves
this day
whom
you will serve.

- Joshua 24:15 -

CHAPTER 11

Seven keys to
miracles,
signs, wonders
and
eternal life!

A SPIRITUAL CURE

There is a distinctly noticeable difference between Constantine's counterfeit Christianity and The Way taught by Christ. The Spirit of God provides abundant evidence of the difference. When the Spirit of God is at work, his work always produces miracles, signs and wonders.

> *For the kingdom of God is not a matter of talk but of power. 1 Corinthians 4:20*

Scripture tells us the natural mind cannot grasp the things of the Spirit. So, predictably, there has not been much teaching about the mighty power of the Spirit of God in Constantine's churchianity and certainly no hands-on training.

> *The natural man does not accept the things that come from the Spirit of God. For they are foolishness to him, and he cannot understand them, because they are spiritually discerned. 1 Corinthians 2:14*

Neither has there been much, if any, teaching about the remarkable nature of God's seven-fold Spirit or how each of his seven Spirits assisted Christ as he did God's work on earth and will help us to do the same work as we follow Christ's Way. In fact, most people who claim to be Christian today don't even know there are Seven Spirits of God, let alone who those Seven Spirits are or what God has sent them to do for the body of Christ.

> *Then I saw a Lamb looking as if he had been slain, standing in the centre of the throne. He had seven horns and seven eyes, which are the seven Spirits of God sent out into the whole Earth. Revelation 5:6*

The Seven Spirits that accompanied Christ on Earth also went with him to the throne room of God after they raised Christ from the dead. From the above Scripture, we see that those Seven Spirits were his crowning glory. They adorned his head as a crown when he took his place as King of Kings.

All in the New Testament!

Contrary to the false Constantinian concept and the erroneous teaching passed down for centuries through Bible Colleges and Seminaries, these seven mighty Spirits of God are not named in the Old Testament, yet each is fully named in the New Testament. Further, each name is accompanied by a description of the specific role of service they have been given to assist those who are filled with the Spirit and follow The Way of Christ.

> *Christ also told them a parable: Can a blind man lead a blind man? Will they not both fall into a pit? A disciple is not above his teacher, but everyone who is fully trained will be like his teacher. Luke 6:39*

These seven Spirits and their roles of service to followers of The Way are not a new doctrine; they are so familiar to you, you will recognise them as soon as you see them listed. They are...

Spirit of Life

His role is to set us free from the Law. *Through Christ, the Law of the Spirit of Life set me free from the Law of sin and death. Romans 8:1-2*

Spirit of Truth

His role is to comfort us and guide us into the truth, which always sets us free. *I will ask the Father, and He will give you another Counsellor to be with you forever–the Spirit of Truth. John 14:15-17*

Spirit of Holiness

His role is to empower the word of God through us and resurrect us on the last day. *...(Christ), who, through the Spirit of Holiness, was declared with power to be the Son of God by His resurrection from the dead. Romans 1:3-4*

Spirit of Adoption

His role is to teach us to take back dominion of the Earth as the children of God. *For you received the Spirit of Adoption. And by him, we cry, 'Abba, Father'. The Spirit himself testifies with our spirit that we are God's children. Romans 8:15-16*

Spirit of Grace

His role is to teach us to revere the great sacrifice Christ made on our behalf. *How much more severely do you think a man deserves to be punished who has trampled the Son of God underfoot, who has treated as an unholy thing the Blood of the Covenant that sanctified him, and who has insulted the Spirit of Grace? Hebrews 10:28-29*

Spirit of Glory

His role is to gently encourage us during times of persecution. *If you are insulted because of the Name of Christ, you are blessed, for the Spirit of Glory and of God rests on you.* 1 Peter 4:14-16

Spirit of Wisdom

His role is to reveal to us the nature of God in everything so that we can know God intimately. *I keep asking that the God of our Lord Jesus Christ, the glorious Father, may give you the Spirit of Wisdom and revelation so that you may know Him better.* Ephesians 1:17

These seven wonderful Spirits were sent to us at Pentecost. They are the keys to the Kingdom, and no force of Hell can prevail against them. All Constantine could do was cement over them—bury them—under the lie that the era of the Spirit, and the miracles, signs and wonders that came with the Spirit was over. He didn't know God!

> *God is not a man, that He should lie or change His mind. Does He speak and not act? Does He promise and not fulfil?* Numbers 23:19

The Keys to the Kingdom

The greatest honour anyone on earth can receive from a Mayor, Governor or King is the key to the city. That key gives its holder the freedom to go wherever they want and enjoy all the city has to offer. What a great and mighty privilege to be given the keys to the spectacular Kingdom of Heaven!

God has not changed His mind about giving us these keys, or about giving us His mighty Spirit, or about empowering the work of Christ through us. These mighty keys are the Way, Truth and Life that Christ carried with him, and they provide us with the bountiful protection of Heaven while we choose to join Christ in doing God's will on Earth.

The full Gospel of Christ!

The best best way to see the full Gospel message of Christ is to study the role and function of the seven wonderful Spirits God sent us to teach, guide, and protect us as we learn to follow Christ's Way.

Typically, Constantinian pulpit preachers tell us we should develop our own character and reputation as a means of attracting people to our church, but that is not what Christ told us to do.

Christ told us to go out in *his name* and the character of *his Spirit* and promote *his Father's reputation*, not ours. He is God's word made flesh. The keys he has passed to us represent his *Name*, *Spirit*, and *Purpose*, and following his lead is how we go in his name to fulfil his Great Commission.

- His name brings the *Life* of our eternal God;
- His name brings the *Truth* about our God;
- His name brings *Adoption* into God's family;
- His name brings the *Glory* of God's favour;
- His name brings the *Grace* of God's protection;
- His name brings the *Wisdom* to know God;
- His name brings the *Holiness* of God's power.

The Spirit of Life...

The *Spirit of Life* breaks the power of legalism and reminds us how and why we were set free, and what we were set free from. As we go out to make disciples, the *Spirit of Life* will assist us in giving personal testimony to the freedom Christ paid for, which now brings us from death to eternal life.

> *Through Christ, the Law of the* **Spirit of Life** *set me free from the Law of sin and death. Romans 8:1-2*

God's goal in sending Christ was the salvation of people. Christ did not die and return from the dead so that a church could be built to commemorate Him. He was not seeking a monument, he was seeking hearts. He sent his *Spirit of Life* to free us from the trappings of religion and all it's laws!

Living in the *Spirit of Life* overcomes the legalistic teaching of apostates who believe that holding to their form of religion and denying the power of the Spirit of God constitutes 'true' Christianity.

The *Spirit of Life* prevents us from falling into the sin of Constantinian clergy who trade eternal life for legalistic works that build their own reputations in this world and grow their denominations. In the end, like unmarked graves, they will have their names permanently removed from living memory.

> *Woe to you because you are like unmarked graves which men walk over without knowing it. Luke 11.44*

The Spirit of Truth...

The *Spirit of Truth* counsels us with the truth to see the reality of worldly works, wealth, ambitions and values so that we can judge our spiritual standing before God by eternal values rather than by the shifting values of the world.

> *I will ask the Father, and He will give you another Counsellor to be with you forever– the **Spirit of Truth**. John 14:15-17*

The wonderful *Spirit of Truth*, empowers our prayers and ensures they reach the throneroom of God. He reminds us that *the gifts and call of God are irrevokable - Romans 11:29* and opens our eyes to the many and various treasures of heaven available to Christ's redeemed.

Living in the *Spirit of Truth* allows us to see that no matter how good our intentions might be, our works will not be complete unless His Spirit empowers them. For God will only reward the works done by the power of His Spirit working through us.

The *Spirit of Truth* prevents us from falling into the sin of the Constantinian clergy who deny the power of the Spirit so that people will depend on them for truth rather than on the Spirit of God.

> *Woe to you because you give God a tenth of your mint, rue and all other kinds of garden herbs, but you neglect justice and the love of God. You should have practised the latter without leaving the former undone. Luke 11.4*

The Spirit of Adoption...

The *Spirit of Adoption* unites us with Christ and God and reminds us that all the redeemed, both male and female, have been set free from the curse that separated us from God and have now been returned to the position held by Adam and Eve before the fall, 100% equal in the eyes of God.

> *For you received the **Spirit of Adoption**. And by him, we cry, 'Abba, Father'. The Spirit himself testifies with our spirit that we are God's children. Romans 8:15-16*

Knowing that we are adopted into the family of God gives us the confidence to use God's name and the name of His Son with authority. As children of the Most High God and the redeemed of Christ, we are privileged to work with them to, once again, take dominion in the same way Christ took dominion.

Living in the *Spirit of Adoption* restores the authority of both men and women to live and work under the powerful covering of the family name.

The *Spirit of Adoption* prevents us from falling into the sin of Constantinian apostates who encourage people to deny the power of the name of Christ and rely on good works to get them to Heaven. The only glory they will ever receive is from the people who bow to their empty pomp and ceremony.

> *Woe to you because you love the most important seats in the synagogues and greetings in the marketplaces. Luke 11:43*

The Spirit of Grace...

The *Spirit of Grace* fiercely defends the sacrifice of Christ and every aspect of the New Covenant that was paid for by his blood. He will never tolerate the trampling of the Gospel and will always empower believers to stand against religious leaders who corrupt the true Gospel of Christ.

> *How much more severely do you think a man deserves to be punished who has trampled the Son of God underfoot, who has treated as an unholy thing the Blood of the Covenant that sanctified him, and who has insulted the* **Spirit of Grace***? Hebrews 10:28-29*

In typical fashion, apostates have changed the meaning of grace and repurposed it to make it mean the same as tolerance. But tolerance insults grace! It is the *Spirit of Grace* who carries out the vengeance of God and of whom it is said, *'It is a dreadful thing to fall into the hands of the living God. Heb.10:30-31.*

The *Spirit of Grace* prevents us from living in the sin of Constantinian apostates, who not only tolerate false teaching but create changes and additions to God's word and pass their misrepresentations to new converts as truth. In the end, they will *fall into the fearsome hands of the living God.*

> *Woe to you, teachers of the Law, you hypocrites! You travel over land and sea to win a single convert, and when you have succeeded, you make them twice as much a child of Hell as you are. Matthew 23:15*

The Spirit of Wisdom...

The *Spirit of Wisdom* takes our hearts and minds beyond the limits of this world, revealing the profound mysteries of God's nature that can be seen everywhere in His creation. While on Earth, Christ continually revealed knowledge of His Father to everyone and asked his followers to do the same.

> *I keep asking that the God of our Lord Jesus Christ, the glorious Father, may give you the **Spirit of Wisdom** and revelation so that you may know Him better.* Ephesians 1:17

In the Old Testament, knowledge of God's might is called the beginning of wisdom *Proverbs 9:10,* and in the New Testament, personally knowing God is our guarantee of eternal life. *John 17:3* The role of the *Spirit of Wisdom* is to help us know God and share our knowledge of the nature of our Father and His Kingdom as we follow Christ's Way.

Living in the *Spirit of Wisdom* protects us from the sin of Constantinian apostates, who make knowledge of God a complex religious chore rather than a functional family relationship. Though they zealously study to learn what has been promised to those who follow The Way of Christ, they reject The Way of Christ themselves and place obstacles in front of those who desire to follow his Way.

> *Woe to you, experts in the Law, because you have taken away the key to knowledge. You yourselves have not entered, and you have hindered those who were entering.* Luke 11:5

The Spirit of Glory...

The *Spirit of Glory* brings God's approval and praise to us during times of persecution. It's not about us praising God; it's about God praising us. During persecution, the *Spirit of Glory* brings God's presence into our lives so powerfully that we experience great joy despite our suffering.

> *If you are insulted because of the Name of Christ, you are blessed, for the **Spirit of Glory** and of God rests on you. 1 Peter 4:14-16*

This is the glory that God poured out on creation when he said, "Ah, it is good!" It is the glory that Jesus experienced at baptism when God said, "This is my beloved son!" It is the same glory that fell on Stephen when he was being stoned to death.

This is the glory bestowed on all those who are persecuted for Christ. The gentle *Spirit of Glory* helps us shun all forms of persecution of others and assists us to endure persecution when it comes to us.

Living in the *Spirit of Glory* protects us from the sin of Constantinian apostates who, for the sake of their religion, actively persecute all who do not conform to their dogmatic ideology or, by their silence, give their consent to the persecutions.

> *Woe to you because you build tombs for the prophets, and it was your forefathers who killed them. So you testify that you approve of what your forefathers did; they killed the prophets, and you build the tombs. Luke 11:47-51*

The Spirit of Holiness...

The *Spirit of Holiness* reminds us that the power we carry is God's power, not ours, and that God's power is made perfect in our weakness. Christ didn't raise himself from the dead, and neither did he do in human strength all the miracles, signs and wonders that accompanied his teaching. The power that flowed through him came straight from the throneroom of God, *the holy of holies,* and he told us we now have access to this same power.

> *(Jesus), through the* **Spirit of Holiness**, *was declared with power to be the Son of God by His resurrection from the dead. Romans 1:3-4*

God's mighty *Spirit of Holiness* will always empower the word of God through every believer so that we can shake off the heavy religious burdens that distract us from obeying Christ, weigh us down, make us subservient, keep us dependant on the clergy class and rob us of our authority to go in Christ's name to fulfil his Great Commission.

Living in the *Spirit of Holiness* protects us from the sin of Constantian apostates, who swap the enormous spiritual power offered to the redeemed for the vague and shifting value of human reputation. Instead of turning people to God, they encourage people to depend on their own limited human efforts.

> *And you, experts in the Law, woe to you because you load people down with burdens they can hardly carry, and you yourselves will not lift one finger to help them. Luke 11.46*

What Constantine didn't understand is that all the miracles, signs and wonders done by Christ during his ministry on Earth were evidence of the power of God's mighty Spirit working through him. If he had understood the spectacular strength and glory of this power and what Christ was offering, he would have sold all he possessed to gain it. But he had no clue! Instead, he stole Christ's name and all his ideas, remade them in his own image, and tried to bury the power of God under a pile of religious rituals, regulations, titles, sacraments and buildings.

God can't be contained!

Today, apostate pretenders in pulpits who rely on their own names and reputations or their denominations' names and reputations show that, like Constantine, they have no desire to go in Christ's name and build the reputation of the Kingdom of God. And also like Constantine, they attempt to bury the power of God still at work in *the priesthood of all believers* under a pile of religious-sounding good works, church activities, study sessions, spiritual snobbery and implied condemnation.

A den of wolves!

> *Such men are false apostles, deceitful workers, masquerading as apostles of Christ. And no wonder, for Satan himself masquerades as an angel of light. It is not surprising, then, if his servants masquerade as servants of righteousness. Their end will correspond to their actions. 2 Corinthians 11:13-15*

Christianity was built using half of Christ's name. It does not represent his full name, which is where his Kingdom authority and power live. Using his half name, some wolves and false prophets perform counterfeit miracles, powered by the devil, to deceive the elect. But these deceptions are always done by those openly 'lording it' over God's people to build personal or denominational reputations.

On the day of judgment, everyone who has chosen this path will say to their judge, *Didn't I do this in your name? Didn't I do that in your name?* And Christ will reply, *Well, actually, no, you didn't!*

> *Many will say to me on that day, 'Lord, did we not prophesy in your name, and drive out demons and perform miracles?' Then I will tell them plainly, 'I never knew you; depart from me, workers of evil!'* Matthew 7:22-23

False prophets are real!

One of the things wolves in sheep's clothing don't want anyone to talk about is wolves in sheep's clothing. False prophets don't want anyone talking about false prophets or rebuking false teaching. Yet false prophets, false teachers and wolves in sheep's clothing are real and can be found in almost every gathering of believers. They are prolific! It is no wonder that Jesus told us he was sending us out as sheep amongst wolves. Constantinian apostates are the perfect example of what false prophets, false teachers, wolves in sheep's clothing, pretenders, religious ogres and the lawless wicked look like.

For false Christs and false prophets will appear and perform great signs and wonders to deceive even the elect, if that were possible. Matthew 13:22

False prophets, false teachers, wolves, religious overlords and pretenders do the exact opposite of the command of Christ and force the redeemed to obey them rather than Christ and the leading of the Spirit. That rebellion is not something God will reward them for on judgment day. For example:

- *Believers:* We should go into the world and preach the Gospel.
- *Religious:* You should come in from the world and listen to us preach to you.

- *Believers:* We should go and heal the sick, raise the dead and cast out demons.
- *Religious:* You're not ready for that yet and should do nothing until we consider you worthy of some less complex ministry.

- *Believers:* Jesus said that when we go out, we should not take any money with us.
- *Religious:* What you really need to do is come in from the world, sit in a pew, do nothing until we say you are ready, and, um, make sure you bring your money with you!

- *Believers:* We think the Great Commission of Christ should be obeyed by everyone.
- *Religious:* It is being obeyed by a select few missionaries whom you can support financially.

Once we recognise what wolves, false prophets, pretenders and religious apostates do, we can no longer pretend we don't know who they are. Once we know, we have the responsibility to make a choice. Will we be silent and go along with the apostasy, becoming apostates ourselves, risking our eternal future? Or will we honour God by walking away from the apostate religion, its advocates and rituals, and choose to follow The Way of Christ?

> *If anyone comes to you but does not bring this teaching, do not receive him into your home or even greet him. Whoever greets such a person shares in his evil deeds. 2 John 1:10-11*

A life-changing decision!

These seven explosively potent Keys of the Kingdom hold all the power we need to walk away from the Constantinian counterfeit. Each of them is a formidable two-edged sword; able to expose and deal with the worst kinds of wickedness while at the same time comforting, healing and leading Christ's redeemed in The Way of righteousness.

The immense power of these keys does not rely on human strength or ability. They come to us, complete, perfect and ready to act, straight from God's throne in Heaven, so that anyone, men, women and children can use them the same way Christ used them. Christ's power was not in his human ability, but in the ability of his Father's Spirit. This is *The Way* Christ wants us to follow. This is how we ensure the will of God is done on earth as it is in Heaven.

Since we
live by the Spirit,
let us walk
in step
with the Spirit.

- Galations 5:25 -

Who Do You Say I Am?

CHAPTER 12

Foot washing,
whip weilding,
boat rocking,
worker of miracles!

THE REPUTATION TRAP

Christ doesn't fit the modern profile of a Christian or society's expectations of what a Christian should be. He was not meek and mild. He didn't bow to the loudest voices or try to make peace with everyone. He was not submissive to authority and didn't always turn the other cheek. He was so bold and blunt that the things he said would today be considered insulting, aggressive, or inflammatory, and so he would not be welcome in most churches.

Christ was not a 'Christian'!

The way Christians are expected to behave today does not line up with anything we see written in Scripture about the one we are supposed to be imitating. And this is because being a Christian bears no resemblance to being a follower of Christ.

Constantine did an excellent job of burying The Way of Christ by confiscating Christ's name, ideas and terminology and recycling them into something that now bears no resemblance to the original. Today, what the world sees and calls Christian is nothing more than the Constantinian counterfeit.

Constantine's brand of Christianity is the product of a false gospel, specifically and elaborately designed to deceive the elect. This is a fact that has not been hidden by history, but is sadly overlooked by adherents of Constantine's deception.

Reputation is a trap!

Through the Constantian counterfeit, Satan was able to place a cleverly camouflaged stumbling block at the feet of every believer. An easy alternative to 'going' in obedience to Christ's Great Commission. This alternative to obedience has been preached continually for hundreds of years from pulpit after pulpit, and the world judges Christians according to its precepts. But it is a lie! This diabolic obstacle is called 'reputation', and it is a deadly trap.

Obey the Great Commission or build a reputation.

The reputation we are encouraged to chase is never placed on us by God. It is always placed on us by people and is constantly changing. It is as fickle and unreliable as a mist, for while we may have a good reputation in one group, we may at the same time be the object of suspicion in another group. Reputation of any kind is an illusion, as shifting and changeable as the sand on the seashore, and can never be trusted to remain intact.

The life of Christ reveals the instability of reputation, for at the same time as the Pharisees hated him, the masses loved him, that is, until the masses suddenly turned on him and began calling for his death. It's a good thing Christ rejected imputed reputation, for whether the reputation he received from people was good or evil, reputation itself didn't phase him. His focus was on his Father.

In the same way that Christ could not avoid gaining a reputation, neither can we avoid gaining one. However, whether the reputation we are given is good for a season or evil for a season, reputation itself is designed to take our eyes off God and place them on ourselves. The only way to overcome the vagaries and confusion of imputed reputation is to do what Christ did and keep our eyes on our Father and obedience to his Great Commission.

Reputation is the greatest deterrent to obedience.

Viewing Christ through the eyes of the Pharisees provides some insight into why they failed to heed his message. They judged him by reputation. In Jewish culture, genealogy was highly regarded, and Jesus had questionable paternity.

- He was born in disgrace; conceived by his mother before his mother was married, then raised by a man who was not his father, except by adoption. His real paternity was unknown.

- His mother and father, though they came from Nazareth in the province of Galilee, chose to live for some time in Egypt, raising their son in isolation from normal Jewish culture.

- Distance prevented his family from being able to encourage Christ to participate in the regular Jewish festivals, feasts, celebrations and temple worship, so it was reasonably understood that he was raised among heathens.

- At twelve years old, Jesus took it upon himself not to go with his parents on their return journey from Jerusalem to Nazareth. His decision caused them great distress, embarrassment and several wasted days in travel. On finding him in the temple at Jerusalem, they mildly chastised him for his inconsideration, but Jesus did not apologise.

- In a society that required rebellious children to be put to death, religious leaders, looking back over the events of Christ's life, could easily consider these actions a serious breach of acceptable behaviour.

- There is no mention of Joseph, Christ's adoptive father, during his ministry, so it is reasonable to assume that he died before it began, and this created another problem.

- As the eldest male in the family, the responsibility to support his mother, brothers and sisters rested firmly on Jesus' shoulders. However, as soon as he was old enough to leave home, Jesus quit the family business and became a vagrant, leaving his mother, brothers and sisters to support themselves—another breach of acceptable behaviour.

- As the Pharisees looked at his life, it appeared that Jesus had become just another irresponsible social dropout; unemployed, living off wealthy women, hanging around with drunks and prostitutes and arguing with authority figures.

- After his unrestrained vandalism of the temple grounds, it was evident to them that he was becoming a problem. It was time to confront him.

- They had looked at his family history, at his family relationships, and at his present lifestyle and associates, and they didn't like the evidence that lay before them. However, it wasn't his family history or his lifestyle and associates that disturbed them; it was what he was saying about their traditions and religious culture that concerned them the most.

- He was becoming dangerous. He was actively provoking people to think about what they believed and why they believed it; about what they did and why they were doing it.

- If he was clever enough, this man of no genealogy, who had been raised amongst heathens, could ruin everything they held dear, their traditions and religious culture.

- Yet they approached him with caution, asking him if he was a prophet or planning to be a revolutionary 'king', after all, they were waiting for a Messiah to lead an assault on the Roman Empire and set Israel free from slavery to Rome.

- Was this the freedom-fighting, prophet-Messiah they had been waiting for? If he laid claim to either of these, prophet or freedom-fighter, they could overlook his unusual ways and lay aside their anxieties to support his mission.

- But, when they confronted him, Jesus did not claim to be either and answered their challenge with a question, *"Who do you say that I am?"*
- The answer was written in their eyes, written in the way they saw him, in what they knew about his family, his lifestyle and his relationships. This irresponsible man could not possibly be the promised Messiah!
- If he was not the Messiah, he could only be a fraud, and if there was no purpose to his dissension, then he was just another troublemaker.
- The subtle approach hadn't worked on him, so the religious community realised they now had no other choice but to take decisive action to control this rebel's influence.
- They decided to kill him and began to look for an acceptable spiritual reason to do so.

It is the same today!

The Pharisees couldn't see God in Christ because they judged by appearances. What they knew about him was more important to them than what he was teaching them about God's Kingdom.

People today still judge by appearances, and what someone shares about the nature of God is filtered through knowledge of their personal acceptability. Many can't see God at work in his people because the reputation of the person is more important to them than knowing God.

For this reason, many believers are deceived into spending their whole lives gaining a good reputation under the mistaken belief that once they are 'good', people will see God in them. But that is just impossible! Being judged by reputation didn't work for Christ, and he was perfect! Why would being judged by reputation work for anyone else?

Gaining a good reputation is not part of following Christ!

Being judged by the unstable vagaries of reputation is as deadly to us as it was to Christ. If Christ were alive today, what would Constantinian apostates do with him? Would today's church leaders accept the opinions of an unqualified social dropout with a dubious past and shady associates, and allow him to question their traditions in front of their congregations? Definitely not! They would do exactly what was done by the Pharisees.

They would examine his family history, his family relationships, his work history, his lack of acceptable religious credentials, his present lifestyle, and his associates, and judge him based on the evidence before them. Then they would find a good spiritual reason to force him to leave their church.

As far as being allowed to preach or teach, it would never happen. Christ would not be regarded as ministry material in most churches today. His lifestyle would put him 'out of the picture'. He would be judged "not Christian enough!" Ironic, isn't it?

Moving beyond reputation!

Christ made himself of no reputation because his ministry was not based on reputation but on the power of God working through him. He deliberately refrained from making himself acceptable to people because he didn't want anyone to praise him for his goodness or for the works he did.

> *Christ did not consider equality with God something to be grasped, but made himself of no reputation, taking on the role of a servant, in the form of a human being.* Philippians 2:7

Adam and Eve fell into sin because they wanted to be like God. They didn't understand that they were already made in God's image, so when Satan told them they could be *'like God, knowing good and evil'* Genesis 3:5 they fell for his lie. What Satan was offering was an illusion; the promise of self-worth that could come from being more like God and therefore equal with God. The desire for a Godly reputation was the sin that ruined everything for all of us.

From the very beginning, Christ totally rejected the sin of Adam and Eve and refused to build his ministry on his personal reputation. His whole ministry was focused on pointing people to the goodness and power of God, and he did this by demonstrating the nature of God in everything he did. The reputation he promoted was his Father's and never his own.

> *I have come not to do my own will, but to do the will of him who sent me,* John 6:38

A study of the Old Testament prophets provides insight into the attitude of mind required to look beyond the trap of reputation. Several of them, Isaiah, Jeremiah, and Ezekiel, were specifically asked by God to disregard the opinions of the people around them and instead do and say what God had told them, despite what anyone else thought.

> *Do not be afraid or terrified of them, though they are a rebellious house. You must speak my words to them, whether they listen or fail to listen, for they are rebellious. But you, son of man, listen to what I say to you. Do not rebel like that rebellious house. Ezekiel 2:6-8*

The Old Testament prophets were always different from everyone around them, and the things they did in obedience to God were sometimes so weirdly unusual that these men could easily be dismissed as madmen.

The people they spoke to had every reason not to listen to them, for they were not what could be called respectable in any way. They dressed in strange clothes, ate unusual food, were often rude, and frequently acted like fools. We know from Scripture that many people did not listen to them, but the humble always listened to their words, repented of their ways and turned back to God.

The behaviour of these men was never meant to be the gauge of their ability to speak the word of God. Further, God expected his faithful ones to look beyond reputation and listen to what was being said.

Only those who were humble enough to look beyond appearances and listen to the word being spoken could hear the message. Those who fell into the reputation trap and judged by appearances, could not hear the message because they stumbled over their own incorrect judgment of the messenger.

It was the same with Christ, and it is the same today. Those who judge by appearances may not hear the word of God spoken by God's imperfect people; nevertheless, God still tells us to go and speak his word to them, whether they listen or not.

It's not about us!

Whether our lives are right in our own eyes or in the eyes of others is beside the point. We are commissioned by Christ to preach the Good News about the Kingdom of God. We are not supposed to 'go' in our own reputation, but in the name of Christ.

The great 'mystery' of the Gospel of Christ is that flesh and blood cannot reveal Christ to anyone. Reputation is mere flesh and blood, and imperfect humans can never do the holy work of God. This is why we have been given the seven spiritual keys to God's kingdom. Only the Spirit of God working through us can reveal Christ to anyone.

Knowing how and when to work with the Spirit to tell people about the Kingdom of God, how to heal the sick, raise the dead and cast out demons takes a knowledge that can't be learned in church or Bible studies. It can only be learned as it is being done.

Whoever listens
to you
listens to me;
whoever rejects you
rejects me;
and whoever rejects me
rejects the One
who sent me.

- Luke 10:16 -

Caesar or God?

CHAPTER 13

How hard
is it to
know what is
Caesar's
and what is
God's?

CHRIST'S WAY

The first disciples of Christ had no credentials, no reputations of their own, no power and no real understanding of how Christ's Way worked. At first, they didn't know Christ was the long-awaited Messiah of Israel. That truth was only revealed to Peter in their third year, so he didn't know who Jesus really was when he was first sent out.

> *Then Jesus called the twelve to Him and began to send them out two by two, giving them authority over unclean spirits. Mark 6:7*

Exponential growth!

As they travelled around, Christ showed his disciples by example how to make disciples, and so what started as a small group quickly grew in number. The next time Christ sent out disciples, there were seventy-two. Like the first twelve, these disciples were not priests. They were not scribes or Pharisees. They were not 'accepted' in religious circles as people who were qualified to talk about religious tradition. They were ordinary workers! Yet Christ sent them out anyway, in his name! His name was their only credential. His name was their only authority. And they discovered fairly quickly that his name carried some hefty supernatural power.

> *The seventy-two returned with joy and said, "Lord, even the demons submit to us in your name." Luke 10:17*

Christ led by example!

When Jesus asked people to join him in proclaiming the truth about the Kingdom of God, he gave them his authority to use his name and then sent them out. If they hesitated, he rebuked them.

> I have kept all God's Commandments," said the young man. "What do I still lack?" Jesus told him, "If you want to be perfect, go, sell your possessions and give to the poor, and you will have treasure in Heaven. Then come, follow Me." When the young man heard this, he went away in sorrow, because he had great wealth. Matthew 19:20-22

> He said to another man, 'Follow me.' But the man replied, 'Lord, first let me go and bury my father.' Jesus said to him, 'Let the dead bury their own dead, but you go and proclaim the kingdom of God.' Luke 9:59-60

Those who went out in obedience experienced, with wonder and awe, the power that comes with the authority of Christ's name. They discovered why this humble man was called *the Word made flesh* as they learned to bring the written Word of God to life in front of their eyes in the same way Christ did.

They didn't go to Bible college first. They didn't even need to spend much time with Christ. He showed them what to do and then told them to go and do the same. It wasn't complicated. They were not relying on their own knowledge or skill. They were not relying on their own goodness. They were totally dependent on the authority of Christ's name.

The disciples didn't always get it right. And Christ was often sharp with them as he rebuked them for their lack of faith. But in front of them, he healed the sick, raised the dead, commanded the wind, walked on water, turned water to wine, fed thousands with two fish and a few loaves, cast out demons, broke Sabbath rules, argued with the religious, shut down the temple, killed a fig tree with a word, appropriated a donkey and foal, and altered time by propelling a boat instantly to the shore.

Everything he did was in demonstration of his Father's authority. His teaching continually extolled the nature of his Father and the glory of his Father's Kingdom. Nothing was done to promote his own reputation or build his own kingdom on earth. He taught his disciples that he was there to represent his Father, and he was sending them out to do the same. They understood that he was not operating in his own authority, but God's, and that it would be the same when they went out. They were not being sent in their own authority, but in God's.

In His Name!

The disciples never heard the name Jesus. That was not the name of the one they followed. The name 'Jesus' was made up 300 years after Christ died. The disciples knew Christ as *Yahoshua*. The same name as the Old Testament leader that was later translated as Joshua. The meaning of this ancient Hebrew name was, *"God, who is salvation"*.

His name is God's name!

The profound mystery of the power of this name is that it is not just Christ's name, but the name of his eternal Father, the name of God himself, for Christ and his Father share the same name. This is why Christ's name is the name above all other names, the most powerful name in the universe!

> *Holy Father, protect them by the power of your name, the name you gave me, so that they may be one as we are one. John 17:11*
>
> *I have come in my Father's name, and you do not accept me; but if someone else comes in his own name, you will accept him. John 5:43*

In the history of the Bible, the only name God has ever given himself is *Yahoshua*, and it was only revealed to the world through His Son. All other names were given to Him by people. At first the disciples didn't know Christ was God's Son, they only knew him as *Yahoshua*. When they were sent out, they went in the name of *'God, who is salvation'*. *Yahoshua* was the first half of Christ's name and it held, and still holds, all the power of God's Authority.

This powerful name represents not only Christ's character but his Father's character and full will for mankind. When combined with second half, *the anointing of the Spirit*, it embodies the entire Gospel. The only credential needed by Christ's first disciples was the willingness to go out, not in their own names or in their own abilities, but in the power and authority contained within this one mighty name.

The only credential needed by us to go out and make disciples is the willingness to go, not in our own names or our own abilities, but in the power and authority of *God who is Salvation.*

His name is his message!

There is no college degree or paper credential that can give us the authority, freedom, power or training that the name of our Redeemer gives. No human credential can make his name 'flesh' in us, or help us love God and our neighbour. No human credential can protect us from the wiles of the devil and his agents or provide us with our own personal testimony to the work of Christ in and through us. No paper credential can authorise us to go in Christ's name and do miracles, signs and wonders, and no human credential can help us face persecution.

Christ's name can do all these things and more, simultaneously!

Christ's name is far more effective than any credential can ever be, and it is a wise believer who looks into the power and authority of Christ's name. Everything we can learn about our Saviour is contained in his name. The message of his life, proven by his death, starts with the Gospel of repentance, which brings salvation and glorifies the name of both Father and Son, *'God, who is Salvation'.*

The Gospel is the power of God for salvation to everyone who believes. Romans 1:16

The word 'anointed' has always meant *'filled with the power of God's Spirit and set apart'*. So, our Saviour's full name carries the authority of *God, who is Salvation,* plus *the anointing power* of God's mighty Spirit. This is why those who are filled with God's Spirit are called 'saints'. Like Christ, we are *set apart as holy* to go in the authority of His Name and the powerful *anointing of His Spirit* to do God's will.

> *All authority in Heaven and on Earth has been given to me. Therefore go... Matthew 28:18-20*

'Salvation' with 'anointing' is the message!

- Salvation from sin through the blood of Christ and the wonders brought by the Spirit's anointing show us how to *overcome everything by the blood of the lamb and word of our testimony.*

- Salvation from sin through the blood of Christ and the wonders brought by the Spirit's anointing show us how the word of God is *made flesh* through us, as it was through Christ.

- Salvation from sin through the blood of Christ and the wonders brought by the Spirit's anointing show us how to bring the *will of God* and the *Kingdom of Heaven* to the Earth.

- Salvation from sin through the blood of Christ fulfils *Christ's command to love God,* and sharing this Gospel of repentance with signs and wonders following is how we fulfil *Christ's command to love for our neighbour as ourselves.*

- Salvation from sin through the blood of Christ and the wonders brought by his Spirit's anointing show us how to preach the *full Gospel message* as we obey *Christ's Great Commission.*

The most powerful name on Earth!

Christ's name teaches us about his divine character, his Father's name, nature and Kingdom, and their combined will of salvation for mankind. It empowers us to do everything Christ has asked his redeemed to do and embodies the entire Gospel. It is the most powerful name anyone can ever access.

It is also comforting to know that if Bibles were suddenly banned or made unavailable, we would still be able to go and fulfil Christ's Great Commission in the same way his first disciples did, because everything we need to know about our amazing Saviour and his message is embedded in his name.

- His name IS his message!
- His name IS his testimony!
- His name IS his Spirit!
- His name IS his commandment!
- His name IS our commission!
- His name IS our authority!
- His name IS our protection!
- His name IS our power to overcome!
- His name IS the word of God!
- His name IS the will of God!
- His name IS the nature of God!
- His name IS the true Gospel!

His name is His Way!

Constantine appropriated the name of Christ and ritualised the ideologies attached to his name. When he stole his name, he thought that as Emperor, Caesar and Pontifex Maximus, he had the authority to change the name's meaning from *God, who is Salvation* to a made-up name with no meaning at all, and designate the use of that new name to an appendage at the end of a prayer. He had no idea that the name he was playing with belonged to the eternal, invincible God. It had a power he couldn't appropriate or understand.

The supreme power of Christ's name is seen in the way God's Word comes alive in the flesh. This is not something Constantine could prevent. Even today, Constantinian apostates don't have the power to make a dent in the truth of God's Word.

Though we know Constantine compiled the New Testament and made additions to suit his new religion, we don't need to be concerned. The only thing that will ever come to life in the flesh is the Word of God, and it is the role of the Spirit to bring the Word of God to life. As we go in Christ's powerful name, the mighty seven-fold Spirit of God will always do the work of Salvation and Anointing, and He already knows what is of God and what is not.

> *No one knows the thoughts of God except the Spirit of God. We have not received the spirit of the world, but the Spirit who is from God, that we may understand what God has freely given us. 1 Corinthians 2:11-12*

The Spirit
searches all things,
even
the deep things
of God.

- 1 Corinthians 2:10 -

Christ's first evangelist!

CHAPTER 14

Should righteous
women
teach, lead, go,
and be
led by the Spirit?

SENDING WOMEN

I shouldn't have to write this chapter, but Constantinian apostates have been working very hard for a long, long time to prevent women from standing in the freedom and authority bought for us by the blood of Christ. It is not logical, rational or spiritual to continue in the false belief that redeemed women are inferior to redeemed men.

Let's start at the beginning...

When God created men and women, he called them "man", which is today called "mankind" or "humankind". This description covers both male and female. There is no separation of concept. Male and female together make up what God calls "man". This means that every God-breathed reference to "man" in the New Testament is speaking of male and female combined. There is no separation of concept. God created "man" as male and female.

> *In the day that God created mankind, he made them in his own likeness. Male and female he created them, and he blessed them. And in the day they were created, he called them "man". Genesis 5:1-2*
>
> *God created man in his own image; in the image of God he created them; male and female he created them. Genesis:1:27*

God made men and women equal! We are still equal!

Then came the fall...

When Adam and Eve sinned against God, they both sinned. They were both equally responsible for the fall of "man" and the subsequent horror story that evolved from their combined decision.

After they sinned, they were both punished by God with punishments that still continue and can be seen at work everywhere today. Men still toil for food, and women still desire to be ruled by males.

> *To the woman. God said: "I will sharply increase your pain in childbirth; in pain you will bring forth children. Your desire will be for your husband, and he will rule over you."*
>
> *To Adam. God said: "Because you have listened to your wife and have eaten from the tree of which I commanded you not to eat, cursed is the ground because of you; through toil you will eat of it all the days of your life." Genesis 3:16-17*

The fall led to the creation by God of a system of laws that, if obeyed, would bring relief in the form of 'blessings', but if not obeyed, would bring extra hardship in the form of 'curses'.

To these laws, various rules and regulations were added by people, such as women covering their hair when they pray or not being allowed to participate in male gatherings. God did not write these extra rules and regulations; they were added to 'assist' women to bow to the will of males as per God's original punishment.

Then God sent Christ. Though Christ called himself the '*son of man*', he didn't have a human father. His only connection to "man" was a woman. This was God's renewed confirmation that males and females, together, make up the concept of "man". For if "man" meant male alone, Christ would not have been able to call himself the '*son of man*'.

> *At that time, they will see the Son of Man coming in the clouds with great power and glory. Mark 13:26*

Christ was sent to us by God to redeem us from the consequences of Adam and Eve's sin and the ongoing tribulation caused by the fall. His redemption would restore "man", both male and female, to the position we had before the fall.

> *For as in Adam all die, so in Christ all will be made alive. 1 Corinthians 15:22*

> *Therefore, if anyone is in Christ, he is a new creation. The old has passed away. Behold, the new has come! 2 Corinthians 5:17*

Redemption from the fall...

The consequence of the sin of Adam and Eve was death, both physical and spiritual, and it applied not just to males but to females as well. Likewise, the consequence of our redemption from death applies not just to males but to females as well.

The role of 'new creation'
applies equally to male and female!

This means redeemed women are no longer under the punishment of God for the sin of Adam and Eve. We are no longer subject to the 'lordship' of men. We are no longer excluded from standing in fellowship with males as equals. Both males and females, through Christ, have been restored to the position God created us to hold, working together with Him to take dominion over His world.

Redeemed means redeemed!

All of you who were baptised into Christ have clothed yourselves with Christ. There is neither Jew nor Greek, slave nor free, male nor female, for you are all one in Christ. Galatians 3:27-28

Righteousness from God comes through faith in Christ to all who believe. There is no distinction, for all have sinned and fall short of the glory of God. Romans 3:22-23

I will pour out my Spirit on all people. Your sons and daughters will prophesy, your young men will see visions, your old men will dream dreams. Even on my menservants and maidservants I will pour out my Spirit and they will prophesy. Acts 2:17

Despite added laws, altered Scriptures, man-made doctrines and the unredeemed relics of male domination, God does not favour males over females. The Spirit of God continues to equip both males and females with all the spiritual tools needed to go in Christ's name to fulfil the Great Commission, which necessarily includes the gift of teaching.

Go and make disciples of all nations, baptising them, and teaching them to obey all I have commanded you. Matthew 28:19-20

Constantine's biggest problem and the reason he founded his pseudo-religion was the unstoppable growth of the Gospel. He knew that disciples were made by teaching and that women love to talk, so the easiest way to stop the spread was to ban women from teaching. It was a simple matter to change a few words in the letters of Paul that he was having translated into Greek. But it was never God's will to exclude women from teaching or going.

On the day of Pentecost, God showed no favouritism to males over females. When he poured out his Spirit, it was onto everyone gathered in the Upper Room. There was no hint that women should remain separate from men or that they could not receive God's Spirit and ministry gifts.

They all met together and were constantly united in prayer, along with Mary, the mother of Jesus, several other women, and the brothers of Jesus. Acts 1:14

When the day of Pentecost came, they were all together in one place. Suddenly, a sound like the blowing of a mighty rushing wind came from heaven and filled the whole house where they were sitting.

They saw tongues like flames of fire that separated and came to rest on each of them. And they were all filled with the Holy Spirit and began to speak in other tongues as the Spirit enabled them. Acts 2:1-4

We receive so we can 'go'!

After he gave his disciples his Commission, Christ told them to wait in Jerusalem until God sent his power. Once they had his power, they would be equipped to *'go into all the world and preach the Gospel'.* On the Day of Pentecost, God gave the promised gift of his power to women as well as men, and it was given so that we could all, male and female, go in his name to do his work.

> *I am sending the promise of my Father upon you. But remain in the city until you have been clothed with power from on high. Luke 24:49*

Equal before God!

The seven-fold Spirit that fell at Pentecost included the *Spirit of Adoption,* who reminds all the redeemed, both male and female, that we have been set free from the curse that separated us from God and have now been returned to the position held by Adam and Eve before the fall. There is no division in this position. Male and female stand side by side as equals before God.

The redeemed are Christ's gift to his Father. He died so that God could once again have fellowship with his children. He tore down the barriers between us, making us one with God. This is now how God sees us, and this is how we need to see ourselves. It is the role of the *Spirit of Adoption* to help us live in this new relationship. If we don't know how to step into it, all we need to do is ask for his help.

Christ's attitude to women!

Christ tore down the barriers between men and women, Jew and Samaritan, while he was on earth. When he visited Jacob's Well, in Samaria, he was met by a Samaritan woman. Not only were Jews not supposed to speak to Samaritans, but men were not supposed to engage other men's wives in conversation, let alone teach them.

As Christ was telling her all he knew about her, this woman realised that this man was not just a prophet, but the promised Messiah. She was the first person in the world to realise Christ was the Messiah.

When she knew who he was, this intelligent woman became so excited that she immediately left her water jar at the well and ran to her town to spread the good news. Many in her town believed her testimony and came out to the well to see the Messiah for themselves. This Samaritan woman was not only the first to recognise Christ as the Messiah, but the first to evangelise a whole town.

The illogical fear that Constantinian apostates added to their 'no teaching' rule was the profoundly vague possibility of 'usurping authority'. My question is, whose authority did the Samaritan woman usurp when she converted her town to Christ? Not only was she encouraged by Christ to go, but usurping supposed male authority wasn't an issue. It was added 300 years later, to curb evangelism and establish the 'authority' of the new clergy class.

Women teach and lead!

Priscilla and her husband Aquilla were teachers and leaders who travelled with Paul to spread the Great Commission. At their home in Corinth, they taught Apollos, who was later known for his depth of Scriptural understanding. Paul's letters to the Corinthians would have been sent to their house.

> *On the Sabbath, we went outside the city gate to the river, where we expected to find a place of prayer. We sat down and began to speak to the women who had gathered there. Acts 16:13*

When travelling through the Roman province of Philippi, the Apostle Paul looked for gatherings of Jews that usually included women. If Paul considered women inferior, or only able to learn from their husbands, he would not have spoken to this gathering of women. It was at this gathering that he met and baptised Lydia and her household. Later, Lydia's home became the central meeting place for believers in Philippi. The letters to the Philippians would have been sent to her house.

Paul's letter to Philemon was addressed to Philemon, his wife Apphia, their son Archipus and the church that met in their house. John's 2nd letter was written to *'the lady chosen by God and her children'*. Women were not only prominent in leading, teaching and enthusiastically following The Way of Christ, but were also founders of many of the first gathering places for believers.

Husbands not required!

Philip was one of the seven who, along with Stephen, were chosen by the twelve Apostles to wait on tables in the first church gathering in Jerusalem. Later, he was directed by the Spirit to go and visit a travelling eunuch and share the Gospel with him.

The eunuch went down into the water and Philip baptised him. When they came up out of the water, the Spirit of the Lord suddenly took Philip away. Act's 8:26-40

After being transported in the Spirit away from the eunuch, Philip travelled to various places until he came to Caesarea, where he settled and made a home. In that place, his four unmarried daughters became well-known as prophets. For them, being unmarried or female was not a hindrance to ministry.

The husband excuse!

In the early church, being unmarried was not a hindrance to receiving salvation or the gifts of the Spirit for ministry. However, being married could often be a hindrance, or worse, if used as an excuse for disobedience. The story of Ananias and Sapphira in Acts 5:1-11 is a definite cautionary tale.

Ananias and Sapphira owned a parcel of land, which they sold. They told everyone the money they received for the land was being donated in full to God's work, but that was a lie. It was that lie, not the amount of money, that got them into trouble.

Peter questioned the husband first, and when he insisted his lie was the truth, the Spirit of God pronounced judgment on him, and he died instantly. A few hours later, his wife, unaware of what had happened, arrived, and Peter asked her the same question. *"Was this the amount of money you received for the sale of the land?"* When she agreed with her husband's lie, she also came under God's judgment for lying to the Holy Spirit, and died.

As God had done with Adam and Eve, the Spirit of God separately gave both husband and wife the opportunity to tell the truth. This tells us that on the day of judgment, husbands and wives will be judged separately. Everyone will be given the opportunity to explain why they didn't obey everything Christ commanded. On that day, being a wife, mother, grandmother, sister, or daughter will not be an excuse for ignoring The Way laid out by Christ.

Testing the spirits!

Although Constantine attempted to crush evangelism by manipulating Scripture, there was one thing he could never control—the might of the Spirit of God. The Spirit of God will always confirm the real Word of God with signs and wonders. This is why we will never see the *Spirit of Truth* stepping in to stop women teaching the Gospel. He will never confirm lies. What Peter did above was test the spirits of Ananias and Sapphira to see if they were genuine or pretenders. The Apostle John asks all believers to learn how to do the same.

Test the spirits
to see if
they are from God,
for many false prophets
have gone
out into the world.

- 1 John 4:1 -

Spirit and Truth!

CHAPTER 15

Apostate teaching brings confusion to those who love Christ!

TESTING THE SPIRITS

The Apostle John was a brilliant teacher. He was able to take all the teaching of the Old Testament about the *abomination of desolation*, all the teaching of Christ about false prophets, and all his personal experience with the *spirit of antichrist,* pinpoint the core problem, find a solution and condense it into one simple teaching; a teaching so simple it could be understood and practiced by a child.

The problem is, the power and wisdom of this simple truth is not taught from pulpits and never will be, because the subject of John's teaching is apostasy and how to identify those who practice it. False prophets, false teachers, religious apostates, wolves in the body and pretenders in the pews will despise this teaching and avoid it like the plague.

> *Dear friends, do not believe every spirit, but test the spirits to see whether they are from God... for many false prophets have gone out into the world... they are from the world and therefore speak from the viewpoint of the world, and the world listens to them. We are from God, and whoever knows God listens to us. John .4:1-6*

The focus of John's solution is exceedingly simple. Pretenders speak from their knowledge of the world about the world. Believers speak from their knowledge of Christ about God and His Kingdom. It's not rocket science. It's not hard to understand.

False prophets can never reveal the beauty and character of God and His Kingdom through their words. They can't explain his nature as Christ did, they can't see parables that glorify God in ordinary day-to-day activities, and they never show how the trustworthy personality of God can be seen in absolutely every single thing he has created on this planet. Instead, they speak of worldly things and give every spiritual truth a worldly application.

For example, they describe how the principles of the Bible can be applied to achieve financial gain or success. They extol the human value of Bible school and church activities rather than the spiritual value of obedience to Christ's Commission. They uphold the apostate worldview that church is about buildings and denominations rather than following The Way of Christ. Not understanding the Kingdom of God, they spend their time explaining church history and the complexities of dogma while the eternal future of the lost is ignored and regarded as far less important than the current fundraiser or coffee morning.

Even the luminous truths contained in the Book of Revelation are given a complex worldview that makes that book seem dark and written about Satanic chaos on earth and the end of the world rather than Christ's glorious final victory over Satan and all his followers. When false prophets, false teachers, wolves and pretenders in pulpits give spiritual concepts a worldly application, they always bring confusion to believers and The Way of Christ.

Powerful protection!

No believer needs to be confused or deceived by false teachers, false prophets, wolves, apostates or pretenders hiding out in the body. The Apostle John's teaching is clear. *This is how we recognise the Spirit of Truth and the spirit of falsehood.* Simply put, to understand if what you are being taught is true or false, use John's test.

It's not difficult to learn how to *test the spirits*, and it can easily become automatic and casually applied to every conversation. John's test never fails, and it can't be faked, for true knowledge of God always has a consequence—it speaks life!

The test is completely inoffensive and so gentle it is undetectable to the one being tested. Applying it places believers in the position of being *wise as a serpent but innocent as a dove, Matthew 10:16.*

All we need to do is listen to the words coming from other people's mouths, for their words will reveal their heart attitudes. If they love the world, they will speak from the viewpoint of the world. If they love God, they will speak about Christ, the glorious character of our Father and his Spirit, and describe the beauty and wonder of his Kingdom.

> *The good man brings good things out of the good treasure of his heart, and the evil man brings evil things out of the evil treasure of his heart. For out of the overflow of the heart the mouth speaks. Luke 6:45*

John's test reflects Christ's teaching that we will know them by their 'fruit' and explains 'how to know them'. By simply listening to the words which come from a person's mouth, the fruit of their own lips, we can know who is of God and who is not.

> *From the fruit of his mouth, a man's heart is filled, and with the harvest of his lips, he is satisfied. The tongue has the power of life and death, and those who love it will eat its fruit. Proverbs18:20-21*

False prophets lie about 'fruit', so despite what many have been taught by wolves in pulpits, knowing who is false by their 'fruit' has nothing to do with miracles, signs, wonders, numbers converted, size of churches, education, houses, success, family relationships, appearances or any other works or deeds, as none of these things bears any resemblance to the long-held Scriptural description of 'fruit'.

All through Scripture, 'fruit' has always meant *the words of the mouth*, which reflect the things we love the most, the things that flow out from our hearts. John's test is the same test God used on Adam and Eve in the Garden of Eden, and it is as effective now as it was then.

God asked Adam and Eve to speak their choice, and when they did, the fruit of their lips revealed their hearts. What God found was that his children were more interested in their own lives and gaining knowledge of the things of this world than in knowing him as a Father. John's test is exactly the same.

So, how do we apply it?

The role of the *Spirit of Truth* is to guide us into all truth, so begin by asking for His assistance. Then check what you have been taught by asking yourself, '*Is this teaching revealing the nature of God and Christ and the beauty of their Kingdom, or is it promoting a human view?*' If the teaching does not promote the Kingdom of God and give glory to both God and Christ, it is not given by the Spirit of God.

Identifying false prophets, wolves, apostates and pretenders, according to Christ's own words, is always done by listening to the words of a person's mouth, not just when a person stands in a pulpit to preach, but in general conversation as well. He assured us that those who seek to promote and uphold the glory of God rather than their own glory can never be regarded as false.

> *Whoever speaks on their own does so to gain personal glory, but he who seeks the glory of the one who sent him is a man of truth; there is nothing false about him.* John 7:18

If we apply this test to all the teaching we hear from pulpits, we will always recognise *apostate doctrine*. If we apply this test to all those who want to influence the way we think, we will never be deceived by *wolves in sheep's clothing*. If we apply this test to every conversation, we will never fall into the trap of living according to worldly standards rather than the Kingdom standards of The Way of Christ.

A clear example!

The whole doctrine of women not being allowed to teach because some man in a pulpit somewhere might get offended is as human and worldly as it gets. It doesn't even come close to passing John's test.

That false doctrine holds no regard for the power of Christ's redemption of women as well as men, or for the need of everyone, male and female, to obey his Great Commission and promote his Gospel by teaching everyone to obey his commands. There is no hint of the tremendous joy in heaven experienced by the Father when he received both sons and daughters back from slavery to sin. That was the joy which enabled Christ to endure the cross, *Hebrews 12:2,* but no, no hint of that joy in this apostate doctrine. All Kingdom truth is denied by this one unholy, man-made addition to God's word. According to John's test, it is a completely false doctrine!

The spirit of antichrist!

John called false teachers, false prophets, wolves and pretenders in the churches, *the antichrist*. He identified their doctrines, beliefs, and deceptions as coming from the *spirit of falsehood*.

The following few verses are the only verses in the entire Bible that mention the word 'antichrist'. They describe who *the antichrist spirit* is in people, how to recognise it, what it will say and do, and how we can overcome it and its deceptions.

> *Dear children, this is the last hour, and as you have heard that the antichrist is coming, even now, many antichrists have come. 1John 2:18*
>
> *Who is the liar? It is the man who denies that Yahoshua is the Christ; such a man is the antichrist. 1John 2:22*
>
> *Dear friends, do not believe every spirit, but test the spirits to see whether they are from God, because many false prophets have gone out into the world.*
>
> *Every spirit that does not acknowledge Yahoshua is not from God. This is the spirit of the antichrist, which you heard is coming and even now is already in the world.*
>
> *We are from God, and whoever knows God listens to us; but whoever is not from God does not listen to us.*
>
> *This is how we recognise the Spirit of truth and the spirit of falsehood. 1John 4:1-6*
>
> *Many deceivers, who do not acknowledge Christ as coming in the flesh, have gone out into the world. Any such person is the deceiver and the antichrist. 2John1:7*

Christ warned his disciples to be on the lookout for the *abomination that causes desolation, Matthew 24:15,* and flee when they saw it. When the abomination turned up, John was the only disciple who didn't flee, for he was willing to die with Christ. Because he didn't try to save his life, he lived longer than other disciples, but in doing so, he saw the abomination up close and was able to give it a name. It was a spirit, and it was as anti-Christ as any antichrist ever gets. So that's what he called it.

John recognised that the *abomination of desolation* and the *spirit of antichrist* were the same thing. The abomination that put Christ to death and the spirit of antichrist, which later tried to destroy the ongoing work of Christ, had the same motive and intention. John taught his disciples to recognise it in people who claimed to be believers but were not.

No antichrist in Revelation!

Another clear example of false doctrine from wolves, false prophets and apostates in pulpits, is the *"last days, Satan in the flesh, single Antichrist world ruler"* scenario. It is a lie from start to finish!

John wrote the Book of Revelation. He also coined the word 'antichrist', yet he didn't include the word 'antichrist' in Revelation. He excluded it! If the writer of Revelation didn't add a scary Antichrist world leader figure into his glorious testimony of Christ, then neither should we. Rather, we should learn from his teaching about the true meaning of 'antichrist' and begin using the word the correct way.

Simple obedience!

It's not our job to understand all false teaching, but it is our responsibility to test the spirits of those who claim to be believers but are not. As we have seen, it is not hard to do. If we keep our eyes on Christ and the beauty of our Father's Kingdom, His Spirit will guide, protect and empower us as we go out in Christ's name to fulfil His Great Commission.

Where
the Spirit
of the Lord is,
there is
freedom!

- Galations 5:1 -

Finally going!

CHAPTER 16

Going
is where
the miracles
live!

LIFE WITHOUT PULPITS

The first disciples had no pulpits. The patriarchs of old had no pulpits. Christ had no pulpit. Instead of pulpits, what they all had was an abundance of miracles, signs and wonders. Honestly, trading miracles, signs and wonders for pulpits is a pretty poor trade, yet that is the trade-off Constantine made when he hijacked The Way of Christ and the half-name of Christ to create his new churchianity.

A world of miracles!

Although the first disciples had no pulpits or Bibles, they understood the power of their Kingdom authority. Yes, they recognised the importance of gathering together with other believers and being faithful in prayer, but they also understood that going out into the world to spread the message of the Gospel was the key to experiencing miracles.

False prophets, wolves, pretenders and various Constantinian apostates in pulpits have convinced believers to disobey Christ's Great Commission, telling us that gathering with other believers for prayer and praise is enough. It isn't! Or the day of miracles has passed. It hasn't! Or that we need credentials before we go. We don't! Obeying Christ's Commission is the only way to shine the light of Christ into this dark world. It is still the only way for people in the world to witness firsthand the authority and power of the Gospel of Christ.

Imagine what it would be like today if billions of God's redeemed suddenly decided to venture out of their church buildings and embrace the Great Commission. God would work with us to unleash His mighty love, salvation, justice, healing, comfort and deliverance over the world *as the waters cover the sea, Habakkuk 2:14*. There would be a massive, worldwide evangelistic explosion, miracles, signs and wonders would flourish, and the true Way of Christ would be seen.

> *People do not light a lamp and put it under a basket. Instead, they set it on a stand, and it gives light to everyone in the house. In the same way, let your light shine before men, that they may see your good deeds and glorify your Father in heaven. Matthew 5:16*

Apostates in pulpits discourage *going into all the world* with words like, 'let's just pray about it', and tell us we are doing all we need to do by attending church one day a week. That is not what Christ meant when he told us to shine our light before men. If that's all we do, then it's exactly what he meant by *putting our light under a basket.* Christ didn't give us his Spirit so that we could hide it under a church building. He intended us to use his Spirit to shine the light of his salvation into the darkness of a confused and hurting world. Going is an action!

Both the Old and New Testaments show that miracles occur when God's people do more than gather and pray; in fact, almost all recorded miracles happened after God's people chose to 'go'.

Abraham and Lot - He chose to 'go'
When Abraham learned that his nephew Lot had been taken captive by a foreign king, he went to war with the king and freed Lot.

Moses and Pharaoh - He chose to 'go'
Moses too action, called down the ten plagues on Egypt, led his people out of Egypt through the Red Sea and met with God on Mount Sinai.

David and Goliath - He chose to 'go'
David's famous battle with the giant soldier from a foreign army, Goliath, was all about taking bold action when the situation arose.

Elijah and Jezebel - He chose to 'go'
Jezebel was a non-believer inside Israel who planted false prophets everywhere. Despite her death threats, Elijah took action.

Samson and Delilah - He chose to 'go'
The greatest warrior Israel had ever seen, Samson, was humiliated by a foreign *femme fatale,* yet God enabled him to defeat the enemy.

Deborah and Sisera - She chose to 'go'
The first female ruler of Israel, Deborah, went to war against an enemy nation. Her killing of the notorious Sisera was a bold action.

Jonah and the Whale - He chose to 'go'
Jonah was sent by God to offer peace to a violent foreign enemy nation. He didn't want to offer them peace, so he ran. God insisted that Jonah do his will. Finally, he chose to 'go' and he saved the city.

There are so many more. I haven't mentioned Queen Esther and Haman, Joshua and the fall of Jericho, Gideon and the Midianites or any of the miracles done by Christ and his disciples as they went out in obedience to the word and God. Going produces miracles. We don't have to just read about them; we can live them. I know, because I have experienced miracles, signs, and wonders, and still do. Miracles, signs and wonders are normal for those who go in faith to follow The Way of Christ.

> *I tell you the truth, anyone who believes in me will do the works I have been doing, and they will do even greater works, because I am going to the Father. You can ask anything in my name, and I will do it, so that the Son can bring glory to the Father. John 14:12-13*

Going is an action of faith!

By Faith, Noah *built* an ark, David *faced* Goliath, Abraham *left his home* and set out to find the promised land, and Moses' parents *broke the law* and hid him from Pharaoh. These were all actions taken before the hope they firmly believed and prayed for was miraculously received.

- Noah believed God's word and acted on it. If he hadn't taken action and built an ark, he would not have seen the miracle of salvation.

- David believed God's word and acted on it. If he hadn't taken the action of challenging Goliath, Israel would not have had a miraculous victory.

- Abraham believed God's word and acted on it. If he hadn't taken the action of leaving his home, he would never have entered the promised land.

Miracles require faith!

Christ encouraged sick people to act in faith. He gave them something to do, and when they obeyed him, they received their miracle. It's the same with us. Christ has given us something to do. He has told us to go, and when we obey him, we will receive our miracle. Sometimes, when people were already doing actions of faith, it allowed Christ to give them a miracle straight away, *'because of their faith'*.

- As a blind man *washed* the mud off his eyes, he was healed. John 9:6-7

- As ten lepers *hurried* to show their diseased skin to the priest, they were healed. Luke 17:11-14

- As a woman *touched* the cloak of Christ in faith, she was healed. Matthew 9:20-22

- When men *lowered* their friend through a roof in faith, he was healed. Luke 5:17-39

Each of these miracles in the Old and New Testaments needed an action of faith to bring it about. The action of 'going' is the common denominator in every one of these testimonies. This tells us that when we go, the action of going will itself be the action of faith needed to bring about the miracles, signs and wonders that result in powerful testimony.

It's time for action!

Confusing the meanings of words was a pivotal component of Constantine's pseudo-Christianity, and 'faith' was one of the words he twisted out of context. In his carefully structured apostasy, 'faith' became merely a substitute word for 'religion' or 'belief', rather than the necessary physical precursor to anointed miracles, signs and wonders, and the doorway to eternal life.

It's no surprise that very few miracles, signs or wonders are seen in the denominational churches today—no one is encouraged to obey Christ's Great Commission! Yet, the action of going in obedience to Christ's command is the only way we can be identified as belonging to *the priesthood of all believers,* and the only way we can fulfil the terms of the New Covenant to gain eternal life. Obedient faith is crucial to salvation! Going in faith, as Christ did, is our call.

Faith is His Way!

The works Christ commands us to do through his Great Commission are actions of faith. They are works that involve preaching the Gospel of repentance, healing the sick, raising the dead, casting out demons and training disciples. We can't do any of these in human strength, yet, when done in the authority of Christ's full name with the power of the Spirit's anointing, our actions of faith will produce miracles, signs and wonders, and result in eternal life—no credentials needed.

This is the narrow road!

When
the Son of Man
returns,
will he find
faith
on the earth?

- Luke 18:8 -

Write the vision!

THE AUTHOR

Write the vision
make it plain,
so that he who
reads it,
will run with it.

- Hab.2:2 -

MONICA BENNETT-RYAN

Hi, I'm Monica!

Thank you for taking the time
to read this little book.

A glimpse into me...

I want to share a testimony that will show how I came to notice the massive difference between The Way of Christ and denominational apostasy. Once I saw God step in and take over, as my father had done for me when I was a teen, everything changed. From then on, no human 'ministry' could satisfy.

Coming out from the Pulpit!

The church was packed. Around three hundred faces looked expectantly toward the podium, waiting for the service to begin. I was behind the pulpit.

I nodded to the pianist, and he led the musicians in the prelude to our first praise song. As was the custom, I moved to the overhead projector, standing about five paces from the pulpit, and placed the first transparency on the lighted surface. While the introduction played, I walked back to the pulpit and gave the call to worship.

This group of people loved to praise, so within a very short time, the presence of God was evident. As the people continued to sing praise, His personal presence among His people intensified until it became like a thick coating of honey that everyone in the building could feel.

Without being instructed, the musicians stopped playing and God's people stood in silent adoration, eyes closed, faces raised to the Lord, open palms held out humbly, in submission.

Then the Holy Spirit took over...

The room was divided into three sections of seats with an aisle between each row. Spontaneously, without any prompting from anywhere, something happened that had never happened before.

The first section began to sing *"Be still and know that I am God..."* soft and reverent until the verse faded and stillness returned; then again, without any prompting, the third section spontaneously took up the second verse while the other two sections remained quiet; when the second verse faded the middle section sang the third verse. Finally, the whole congregation joined in for the finale.

Led by an invisible choirmaster, the presence of God saturated the atmosphere. His presence was more intense than I had ever felt in my life, and I was a spectator, watching dumbstruck at what God Himself was doing with His people.

Then the Spirit spoke...

A voice began to speak loudly in tongues, and I knew that this was a tongue that needed interpretation, or it would be out of order. I understood what the tongue was saying, so when it finished, instead of blurting out my understanding, I waited for someone else to bring the interpretation. I didn't need to wait long.

A woman began the interpretation, and hers was the same as mine, but about a third of the way through, she suddenly stopped speaking. Her mouth was open, but she couldn't continue.

The pianist, with his eyes closed, continued as if there had been no break in the interpretation, and I knew that what he was saying was correct.

Then, as suddenly as the woman had stopped speaking, he also stopped, mid-sentence, like his mind had just gone blank, so I finished his sentence and the rest of the interpretation.

Everyone remained in adoration. You could hear a pin drop. I suddenly remembered that I was supposed to be leading the praise, and believed it was up to me to ensure that this wonderful sense of God's presence stayed a little longer.

The next prepared song flowed beautifully with the mood and the prophetic word that had been given, so I decided to signal the musicians to begin playing, but first, I needed to put the overhead transparency in place. No one was watching me. All eyes were closed. Nobody knew what was in my mind except God himself.

Behind the wooden pulpit, I lifted my foot ever so slightly to begin walking unobtrusively toward the projector. I didn't want to do anything to distract anyone from the powerful presence of God.

A gentle rebuke...

Before I could take that first step, before I had put my foot down, God rebuked me! A voice called loudly from the congregation, *"Do not be too hasty to move out of my presence!"*

I froze! My foot was still raised, but my eyes flew open to see who had spoken the words. I was too late. Every eye was closed, and everyone continued in the presence of God. Not one single person knew that I had been rebuked. But I knew.

Even though I had been watching God move, seeing Him, as physically as possible, enter into the praises of His people, I had arrogantly assumed that He needed my help. I was so wrong! God didn't need my help. He was capable of doing anything He wanted to do with His people, and I was about to get in His way. It was clear that He had planned something more, and I was about to interfere and possibly quench His Spirit. Thankfully, he had no intention of letting me.

I needed to repent...

I immediately felt small, tiny, as you tend to feel when God rebukes you, and I had an overwhelming desire to kneel before Him and repent, not just for being in His way, but for other things as well. I was no longer a leader; I was his child.

I left the podium, joined the congregation and knelt facing the pulpit I had abandoned. I ignored everyone around me and repented quietly. No one heard my prayer. When I looked up about ten minutes later, the whole church was in repentance! People were crying, kneeling, standing, praying with one another, hugging, repenting alone, or lying prostrate in the aisles before God.

The thing that struck me most was the continued quietness. The room was filled with the presence of God and the powerful emotions of people confessing their sins to Him and to one another, repenting with tears, yet the quietness was overwhelming.

I knew God had done what He wanted to do, so I went back to the pulpit, brought the praise to a close and handed the service over to the minister.

Then came the downside...

I was married to that minister, a wolf in sheep's clothing, and the worst kind of pretender. Before my father died, I had told God I was ready for *the wicked to surround me and try to steal my soul*. After my father died, God took me at my word, and I was soon surrounded by wolves, and living with one.

I knew my husband wouldn't like what had just happened. He would think that I was trying to upstage him, usurp his position and become more popular. He had no idea that all glory for ministry belonged to God. He thought the glory should be his.

I say about him what Paul said about Alexander the Coppersmith, *"He did me much harm!"* 2Timothy 4:14. My husband was homosexual, hated women, was hedonistically cruel and violent, lied about everything, slandered all who challenged him and was, in later life, arrested and charged with pedophilia. Being married to him revealed the 'inside story' of denominational ministry, for I found it didn't matter how evil this man was, the other wolves protected him, and still do.

The morning service had been glorious, and I was due to lead the praise again at the night service, but I could feel the unspoken tension in my husband rising as it always did before he beat me.

About half an hour before I was due to leave for the service, his fury and hatred exploded out of him in one of his typical violent rages. When he finished beating me, I was a mess, visibly shaking, crying, and struggling to get my emotions under control. I knew I couldn't lead the praise, but when I told him I was not fit to lead praise, he insisted I lead, and threatened more violence if I didn't.

That's when I realised, he didn't want what had happened in the morning service to be repeated. He didn't care that God Himself had shown up and led the praise. He was only afraid people would seek me out instead of him, and he couldn't allow that.

He wanted to humiliate me...

I was grateful to be alone as I headed to the service. It gave me the much-needed space to talk to my Lord, forgive my husband and hand everything over to God. When I entered the church, I felt detached from people because I was trying to hold myself together. I was still shaking. I guess medically speaking, I was still in shock. Though I had forgiven him, I was still trying to recover from my husband's vicious beating.

I knew I should not be leading the praise. I was far too emotional. And with emotions screaming at me, I could not be sensitive to what God wanted to do.

When I stepped up to the podium, the music began, and I took the microphone. The faces looking at me were expectant; they wanted more of the glory they had experienced that morning. For the second time in one day, I was in danger of standing in God's way. I wanted to be honest, expose the violence I had just encountered and ask for prayer, but that too would interfere with praise. So I said nothing. I didn't know back then what I know now. I needed to learn.

I opened my mouth to sing, and my voice cracked. I couldn't sing. I breathed a sigh of thanks to my gracious Lord for not allowing me to block Him and for giving me a way out. I motioned to one of the singers to take over and stepped down from the podium. My husband was standing at the back of the church, glaring at me with a smug smile and hatred in his eyes. Like Constantine, he had trampled true worship and was now back in control, or so he thought...

As a child, I was made aware of ogres in the churches, and as a teenager, I stood against a false prophet. Now, though living in a wolf's lair, my Lord had just given me a beautiful cameo keepsake. In one day, God carved out for me an exquisite raised impression of the Spirit of God at work in His people, starkly contrasted against a dark backdrop of wolfish apostasy seeking to veto the work of God's Spirit. That cameo brought everything into focus.

> *Those controlled by the flesh cannot please God. And if anyone does not have the Spirit of Christ, he does not belong to Christ. Romans 8:8*

Some related reading...

CONSTANTINE VERSES CHRIST:

Dr Alistair Kee argues that Constantine was not a Christian, for to Constantine, religion was part of an Imperial strategy. Using Christianity for his own ends, Constantine succeeded in replacing the norms of Christ and the early church with the norms of Imperial ideology.

https://www.amazon.com.au/Constantine-Verses-Christ-Triumph-Ideology/dp/149829572X

THE ANTICHRIST DECEPTION

When the Imperial Roman regime ended, it didn't disappear entirely but took on a different form and subtly continued to influence the world. Now it proudly promotes itself as the New World Order.

https://www.amazon.com/ANTICHRIST-DECEPTION-Monica-Bennett-Ryan-ebook/dp/B0CP7JTNTD

REVELATION: ANCIENT AND MYSTERIOUS

Disclosing how Christ's powerful death culminated in an even more powerful resurrection, this book obliterates the false Satan-glorifying horror-story worldview. Taking the mystery out of the perplexing vision of the ten-horned beast, his mark and number, the second beast and the woman that accompanies them, the author explains the amazing roles of the seven Spirits, four living creatures, two witnesses and three demonic frogs, and brings to life the heart-pounding imagery of the four horsemen, seven seals, armageddon and the end of the world.

https://www.amazon.com.au/Revelation-Ancient-Mysterious-Monica-Bennett-Ryan/dp/0645351342

Why I wrote this book...

Now free to follow Christ, I love to sit with a cup of coffee and my Bible and *write the vision* that God puts on my heart. I have penned several books, and they usually take years to write. The first took decades.

This book was different!

I didn't know I was going to write this book. I woke up one day and thought, "I really need to write down some of the things I've been thinking about and living since childhood". When I started to write, it flowed continually and didn't stop. From the time I decided to write it to its completion was four weeks. I was amazed. I've never written a book so fast.

I knew the subject, I'd lived it. I'd done the research over many years. The testimonies were piled up, and it was just a matter of asking the Spirit of God which ones to use and how to write each chapter.

I felt an urgency to write this book, as if God were planning a worldwide evangelistic explosion that would soon reverberate across the earth, filling the world with new believers who would not be satisfied with Constantinian churchianity or settle for mere Sunday service ritual.

These new believers would seek a genuine relationship with Christ and would need to know that it was okay to trust His Spirit and simply 'go', without denominational credentials, to make disciples for Christ by following The Way of the first disciples.

If you identify with this vision,
God bless you, this book is for you.

Coming to Judge!

Come out of her
my people,
so that you
will not
share in her sins,
and receive
her punishments.

- Revelation 18:4 -

www.ingramcontent.com/pod-product-compliance
Lightning Source LLC
Chambersburg PA
CBHW051422290426
44109CB00016B/1398